Branded Entertainment in

Branded Entertainment in Korea examines the varied texts and wider context of branded entertainment and related advertising and marketing communications practices in Korea.

The book discusses the origins, development, current state, ethics, and regulations of branded entertainment in Korea, considering the impact and implications for communication users and regulators as well as industry actors. Over 30 cases from 2013 to 2019 are offered to provide an up-to-date account of current developments, with a closer look at the ethical challenges and controversies surrounding branded entertainment. The book also provides a review of branded entertainment-related literature in order to help the readers to understand this growing marketing discipline.

This is a valuable case study for scholars and students of critical advertising studies, as well as those interested in broader disciplines of communication and media studies.

Hyunsun Yoon is Senior Lecturer in Advertising and Marketing Communications in the Faculty of Business at the University of Greenwich, UK. She has researched and published on the subjects of advertising, communications, ageing consumers and the Korean wave. Recent projects include digital vulnerability and empowerment among older consumers.

Routledge Critical Advertising Studies

Routledge Critical Advertising Studies tracks the profound changes that have taken place in the field of advertising. Presenting thought-provoking scholarship from both prominent scholars and emerging researchers, these ground-breaking short form publications cover cutting-edge research concerns and contemporary issues within the field. Titles in the series explore emerging trends, present detailed case studies and offer new assessments of topics such as branded content, economic surveillance, product placement, gender in marketing, and promotional screen media. Responding quickly to the latest developments in the field, the series is intellectually compelling, refreshingly open, provocative and action-oriented.

Series Editor: Jonathan Hardy

Alternative Reality Games
Stephanie Janes

Branded Entertainment and Cinema
The Marketisation of Italian Film
Gloria Dagnino

Branding Diversity
New Advertising and Cultural Strategies
Susie Khamis

Branded Entertainment in Korea
Hyunsun Yoon

For more information about this series, please visit: www.routledge.com/Routledge-Critical-Advertising-Studies/book-series/RCAS

Branded Entertainment in Korea

Hyunsun Yoon

Routledge
Taylor & Francis Group

LONDON AND NEW YORK

First published 2021
by Routledge
2 Park Square, Milton Park, Abingdon, Oxon OX14 4RN

and by Routledge
52 Vanderbilt Avenue, New York, NY 10017

Routledge is an imprint of the Taylor & Francis Group, an informa business

British Library Cataloguing-in-Publication Data
A catalogue record for this book is available from the British Library

Library of Congress Cataloging-in-Publication Data
Names: Yoon, Hyunsun, author.
Title: Branded entertainment in Korea / Hyunsun Yoon.
Description: London; New York: Routledge, 2020. |
Series: Routledge critical advertising studies |
Includes bibliographical references and index. |
Summary: "Branded Entertainment in Korea examines the varied texts
and wider context of branded entertainment and related advertising and
marketing communications practices in Korea. The book discusses the
origins, development, current state, ethics and regulations of branded
entertainment in Korea, considering the impact and implications for
communication users and regulators as well as industry actors. Over thirty
cases from 2013 to 2019 are offered to provide an up-to-date account of
current developments, with a closer look at the ethical challenges and
controversies surrounding branded entertainment. The book also provides
a review of branded entertainment related literature in order to help the
readers to understand this growing marketing discipline. This is a valuable
case study for scholars and students of critical advertising studies, as well as
those interested in broader disciplines of communication and media studies"–
Provided by publisher.
Identifiers: LCCN 2020027703 | ISBN 9780367205317 (hardback) |
ISBN 9780429262043 (ebook)
Subjects: LCSH: Branding (Marketing)–Korea (South) |
Mass media–Korea (South)–Marketing. |
Business communication–Korea (South)
Classification: LCC HF5415.1255 .Y66 2020 |
DDC 338.4/7790095195–dc23
LC record available at https://lccn.loc.gov/2020027703

ISBN: 978-0-367-20531-7 (hbk)
ISBN: 978-0-429-26204-3 (ebk)

Typeset in Times New Roman
by Newgen Publishing UK

Contents

Acknowledgements   vi

Introduction   1

1   Media and advertising in Korea   15

2   Branded entertainment: literature review   28

3   Branded entertainment in practice   39

4   Issues, challenges, and prospects   59

Index   75

Acknowledgements

I would like to thank my series editor, Jonathan Hardy, who has been extremely generous with his time and feedback for this book. I am also deeply grateful to Guiohk Lee for her insightful suggestions. My sincere thanks go to Helen Powell and Jongsoo Lee for their friendship and advice. I wish to thank all those colleagues, friends, and students who have provided advice, encouragement, and examples, including Hyunsoon Park, Tina Segota, Heonkwan Jeong, Donghee Choi, and Hyungjun Choi. I would also like to extend my gratitude to the editorial team at Routledge, especially Priscille Biehlmann for her patience and support. I would especially like to thank my first PhD supervisor, Professor John Hartley, for his enduring support and guidance for over two decades. Last but hardly least I am deeply indebted to my family – my parents, Kyonghwa, Woosang, and Siobhan – for their unwavering support.

Introduction

Calling all fans, lovers of #Hyundai and #BTS, if you happen to be in London next Friday, come witness the 1-hour exclusive of our journey with BTS on the world's most iconic screen at Piccadilly Circus. You don't want to miss it, so mark your calendars: 31 May, from 6–7pm.

(Hyundai Worldwide, 2019a)

South Korean carmaker Hyundai's Twitter feed promoted a never-before-seen one-hour-long video of the boy band BTS. Unveiled the night before BTS's concert at Wembley Stadium was the new advertising campaign for Hyundai's SUV Palisade. Hyundai tweeted BTS fans and the general public to post a photo/video of this on Instagram or Twitter and tag #hyundai.lifestyle to win a prize (Hyundai Worldwide, 2019b). It had over 200k likes and nearly 50k retweets at the time. This is an example of how Hyundai engages with consumers through branded entertainment. Hyundai has followed many other car brands that have used branded entertainment in the last two decades. Ford's *No Boundaries* series (2001), BMW's *The Hire* series (2001/2002), Mercedes' *Lucky Star* (2002), and Honda's *Honda Cog* (2003) are good examples (Grainge, 2011: 178). In the Korean context, carmakers were one of the first brands to use branded entertainment, in particular, branded films, in their promotional mix, for instance, Kia's Lotze *Identity* (2006) and SsangYong Motor's *U-turn* (2008).

This book examines the wider context and varied texts of branded entertainment and related advertising and marketing communications practices in the Republic of Korea (hereafter, Korea). It discusses the origins, development, current state, ethics, and regulations of branded entertainment. Despite increasing interest from media companies and consumers worldwide, the way that the Korean media and marketing industries work and engage with branded entertainment is not yet well understood in the English-speaking world. This book provides an up-to-date account of current developments, with a closer look at the legal and ethical issues surrounding branded entertainment. The book also offers a review of branded entertainment-related literature in order to help the readers understand this growing marketing discipline. Situated in Critical Advertising Studies, this book addresses wider criticisms such as the legitimacy and accountability of branded entertainment. It also raises questions around ethical challenges and controversies rather than just representing a marketer's operational perspective on branded entertainment's role in the marketing mix. The book contributes to critical advertising studies by considering the impact and implications for communication users and not just the industry actors. It explores the ways in which the Korean media and marketing industries engage with branded entertainment by considering critical issues.

For the most part, the inception of branded entertainment is a response by the advertising industry to a digital search culture that has unsettled promotional methods and business models based on spot commercials (Grainge, 2011: 176). According to the Motion Picture Association, the number of subscriptions to online video services around the world increased to 863.9 million (+28 per cent) and more than three-quarters of adults watched movies and TV shows via online subscription services in 2019. More than 85 per cent of children and 55 per cent of adults watched movies and/or TV shows on their mobile devices (WARC, 2020). These changes enabled more and more viewers to avoid advertising. Integrating advertising into programmes has been regarded as a solution to two problems: the declining reach and effectiveness of TV 'spot' advertising, and the rising costs of programme production (Hardy, 2010: 238). Embedding promotions in media contributes to combatting advertising avoidance. As the effectiveness of traditional advertising formats declines, branded entertainment is becoming more popular (Appleyard, 2010; DeMers, 2016). Branding, once a nascent marketing discipline, continued to grow, and global branded entertainment marketing revenues rose 8 per cent to $106.2 billion in 2017, fuelled by the ninth consecutive year of double-digit growth in product placement and consumer content marketing worldwide (PQ Media, 2018).

'Shoppertainment' is a term coined by Lazada, an Alibaba-owned e-commerce company in Asia, meaning 'innovations that merge shopping with entertainment and social experiences by which consumers watch, play and stay' (Lim, 2020). At the time of writing this book, many people are either in lockdown or social distancing due to the global pandemic (COVID-19). This is affecting the way we consume media (Charton, 2020) and also, more people are using livestreaming to socialise with each other and with brands. So-called shoppertainment, in many ways, resembles convergence and a multifaceted relationship we have in engaging with media, goods, and people. According to Hardy (2018: 116), media and marketing integration is arguably the next phase of convergence, following that of the convergence of mass media, telecommunications, and computing. Marketers are becoming broadcasters and publishers, whilst the media is increasingly incorporating brand-created or sponsored content (Hardy, 2018: 103). Critical concerns for such media-marketing convergence include the issues of disclosure, consumer awareness, integrity of communications channels, and creative autonomy. This book aims to address these concerns, with the goal of contributing to critical scholarship.

What is branded entertainment?

Branded entertainment has been regarded by marketing practitioners as a way to successfully reach and engage consumers and to build a strong emotional relationship with them (Hudson and Hudson, 2006; Choi et al., 2018). Yet the definition of branded entertainment is still vague at best (Raunio and Arhio, 2015). While there is no uniform definition, various scholars have attempted to define branded entertainment. Some academics and practitioners see branded entertainment as product placement, product integration, and sponsorship (see Russell and Belch, 2005; Hudson and Hudson, 2006; Van Reijmersdal, Neijens and Smit, 2007; Lehu, 2009; Kunz, Elsässer, and Santomier, 2016; Turow, 2016). For example, Hudson and Hudson (2006: 492) defined branded entertainment as 'the integration of advertising into entertainment content, whereby brands are embedded into storylines of a film, television program, or other entertainment medium'. Similarly, Turow (2016: 111) states that branded entertainment is 'the act of linking the firm or product's name and personality with an activity that the target audience enjoys', and that it is an activity which belongs to integrated marketing communications or just marketing communications. From this perspective, the three most common forms of branded entertainment are event marketing, event sponsorship, and product placement (Turow, 2016: 111).

In contrast, other practitioners and academics consider branded entertainment to be a brand-generated communication initiative, not product placement or integration (see Caraccioli-Davis, 2005; Bhargava, 2011; Chen and Lee, 2014; Valero, 2014; Woodrooffe, 2014;

Raunio and Arhio, 2015). In other words, they argue that the brand should generate the entertainment and *hence control a sense of full ownership* (Van Loggerenberg, Enslin, and Terblanche-Smit, 2019: 4). Yet another school of thought is of those who are relatively vague on ownership, with a more all-encompassing view of branded entertainment (see Spurgeon, 2008; O'Guinn, Allen, and Semenik, 2009). For example, O'Guinn, Allen, and Semenik (2009: 612) define branded entertainment as 'the development and support of any entertainment property where a primary objective is to feature one's brand or brands in an effort to impress and connect with consumers in a unique and compelling way'. Similarly, Spurgeon (2008: 40) claims that unlike sponsorship and product placement, which affiliates brands with existing film and television vehicles, branded entertainment involves the creation of content that contextualises 'brand images in ways that are so appealing that consumers will seek them out for inclusion in their personalized media and entertainment flows'.

Hence, three different takes on branded entertainment can be identified: first, branded entertainment as product placement and integration; second, branded entertainment as brand-generated content with full ownership and control of intellectual property; and third, brand integration but only with uncertain or partial control and ownership. For example, an earlier study by Hudson and Hudson (2006) proposed that in branded entertainment content, the brand or products are integrated into entertainment content that is *created and distributed by* the brands themselves [emphasis added]. However, not all branded entertainment fits the description. Content creation can be by the brand, or by others (such as production companies) on behalf the brand, or by a collaboration between more than one brand (i.e. Dubai Tourism's partnership with Red Bull; Tusing, 2019). Even so, not all branded entertainment is distributed by the brands themselves. For example, outdoor clothing company Patagonia's documentary film *Artifishal* was distributed via Netflix (McCarthy, 2019).

More recent studies from Hardy (2018), Van Loggerenberg, Enslin, and Terblanche-Smit (2019), and Dagnino (2020) acknowledge that various definitions of branded entertainment exist with very trying perplexities spanning extremes in explanations, interpretations, and applications. Hardy (2018: 109) also emphasises the ongoing diversification of platforms: 'terms such as product integration and branded entertainment highlight the move beyond simple placement into more sophisticated, and extended, brand presence [...] product placement has also enveloped a range of other entertainment media forms, including computer games (advergames)'. In a synthesis of the above definitions, three issues can be identified: content creation, ownership, and control. Van Loggerenberg, Enslin, and Terblanche-Smit (2019) conducted interviews with planners and creators of branded entertainment campaigns in the global context and proposed the following definition: 'Branded entertainment is a communication effort that employs a compelling authentic narrative to achieve brand resonance'. However, this definition does not explain ownership or control as much as it does content creation. In this regard, Dagnino (2020: 22) captures the complexities around these issues well when she defines 'branded entertainment as a genre-specific form of branded content that consists of any entertainment product, most frequently in the video format, originally produced and *creatively controlled* by an advertiser' [author's emphasis].

Overall, the lack of a cohesive understanding and application is concerning because branded entertainment is growing in importance as a means to disrupt conventional communication practice (Van Loggerenberg, Enslin, and Terblanche-Smit, 2019). While some argue that branded entertainment marks a fundamental shift from intrusive advertisements pushed at audiences who are engaged in other content to advertising of such merit or interest that the audience actively seeks it out (Donaton, 2004; Donaton 2007; Lotz, 2007: 172), it is essential that we unravel overlooked concerns such as ownership, control, integrity, and authenticity. By doing so, one can verify whether this is a fundamental shift or just a newer form of conventional promotional strategies. This book aims to do so by exploring one emerging market, Korea. The next section explains why and how this book came to be written.

A research/knowledge gap in Korean advertising

According to the Korea Advertising Association and Media Audit Korea, Korea's advertising market was the sixth largest in 2017 among member nations of the Organisation for Economic Co-operation and Development. Total media advertising spending in Korea reached $10 billion in 2018, up 4.6 per cent over the previous year. There are over 3,000 agencies which consist of both the foreign and domestic kind (Ministry of Science and ICT and Korean Broadcast Advertising Corporation (KOBACO), 2018). Despite its size and continual growth, there is a noticeable lack of book publications in English about Korea-related advertising research, while the major venues for spreading knowledge have been academic journals. Although there is one book in English written by Shin and Shin (2013), titled *Advertising in Korea*, it was published and distributed by a Korean publisher, Communication

Books, so the readership seems to have remained primarily within Korea. Jeong and Kim (2018) examined a survey of the articles that addressed Korea-related advertising research published between 1990 and 2016 in major advertising, marketing, and communication journals. They found that despite a continuous increase in the number of advertising research studies about Korea and Asia in general over the years, extant research is still lagging behind industry developments. For example, in 2018, Korea's digital advertising reached $4.6 billion (approximately £3.6 billion), growing by 16 per cent compared to the previous year (Ministry of Culture, Sports and Tourism, 2019) and yet existing studies rarely covered digital advertising in Korea.

The lack of writing in English has meant that there is a poor understanding or even a neglect of the Korean media system. Furthermore, the focus of writing on Korean advertising tends to be specific and affirmative, examining various promotional tools and the effectiveness of them, and the quantitative approach has been dominant in Korea-related advertising research (Khang et al., 2016; Jeong and Kim, 2018). Existing research tends to be affirmative in that it adopts and endorses the governing concerns of industry actors in formulating research questions. By contrast, critical research serves to address societal structures and institutions that oppress and exclude so that transformative actions can be generated which reduce inequitable power conditions (Steinberg and Cannella, 2012). For example, the ideological consequences of integrated advertising serve to maintain consumer ignorance about the social relations about brands and propagate the hegemony of consumerism (Spurgeon, 2015: 73). However, current literature on Korean advertising tends to focus more on actual practices than on these consequences and implications, especially on 'vulnerable' consumers who have less media and digital literacy to discern commercial consideration for content. Thus, there is a gap to fill by adopting critical research.

There are several reasons why it is important and timely that media, advertising, and marketing in Korea should be better understood. First of all, Korea is one of the most wired countries in the world (BBC, 2016; Lankov, 2019). Internet penetration among the Korean population increased rapidly, and by 2018, 98 per cent of the entire Korean population (43.94 million) were internet users (Ministry of Science and ICT and KOBACO, 2018). Since the mid-1990s, Korea's economic growth has relied on the information technology (IT) industry and the Korean government has pursued a policy of high-speed telecommunication infrastructure as a foundation to build a 'knowledge-based society'

(Ryu, Kim, and Kim, 2003: 6–7). The government started work on an initial plan for the Korea Information Infrastructure (KII) in 1993 and set up a comprehensive plan in March 1995 (Korea Information Society Development Institute (KISDI), 2001). In August 1995, *The Basic Law for the Promotion of the Information Society* was enacted to drive the nationwide KII project (Ryu, Kim, and Kim, 2003: 7). Following this, the *Basic Plan* proposed several telecommunications reforms from 1996 to 2000, which emphasised competition and deregulation (Ministry of Information and Communication (MIC), 2003). The Korean government has pursued telecommunication policies for competition, based on deregulation and market principles. The internet market was not an exception. Broadband internet service was initially classified by the Korean government as a value-added service, and therefore was free of regulation regarding entry and pricing (Oh and Larson, 2011: 88). Free entries to the market enabled lower prices. It is noteworthy that Korea achieved broadband internet success without local loop unbundling[1] (Oh and Larson, 2011: 88). The fact that the Korea Electric Power Corporation's (KEPCO's) fibre optic network reached most of the nation's high-rise apartments where a large proportion of the population lived, meant competitive suppliers could readily gain access to transmission facilities (Oh and Larson, 2011: 88).

Secondly, there is a significant need for research about changing relationships between marketing communications and media in developing countries. Relative to the developed countries, developing countries are neglected (Eagle and Dahl, 2015). There is a tendency amongst industries and academic researchers to extrapolate supposedly global patterns based on studies of conditions that are not replicated in developing countries. Therefore, there is a need to examine commonalities across developing countries as 'small states' research does in media systems studies (see Hardy, 2012; Picard and Russi, 2012). In the 1990s, as Korean media culture became more sophisticated, conventional communications tools such as traditional TV advertising via commercials faced increasing limitations (Chae and Sun, 2013: 55). However, what was distinctive in the Korean case was the role played by the state in culture industry, especially in the audiovisual sector and the new media sector. For example, in 1995, the Korean government enacted the *Motion Picture Promotion Law*, which encouraged business conglomerates (*chaebols*) to invest in the film industry to boost cultural exports (Kim, 2013: 4). In the online gaming industry, while Western countries and Japan have emphasised console games, it was the Korean government's policy to develop and export online games (Jin, 2013: 151).

As new digital media such as the internet and satellite broadcasting have entered the scene, businesses have deemed it necessary to establish more integrated marketing communications. Agencies specialising in product placement and integration emerged in the early 2000s (Chae and Sun, 2013: 55). The revised *Broadcasting Act* was proposed by the legislature in December 2008 to add product placement to the Act and the revised bill of the enforcement ordinance of the Act was approved in 2010, 'allowing' product placement in terrestrial broadcasting and cable channels (Korea Communications Commission, 2010). There is no mention of branded entertainment, but product placement is defined by the current *Broadcasting Act* (Article 73)[2] as 'commercials that expose products, trademarks, names or logos of companies or services and others within broadcast programmes' (Korea Ministry of Government Legislation, 2020).

Lastly, the Western creative industries could learn from the development of branded entertainment, with a special reference to Korea's recent success in the popular culture export industry. Small states' media systems generally reach small audiences, but the so-called Korean wave (*Hallyu*) has been a widely recognised phenomenon over the last two decades. There are a number of academic books and articles on the Korean wave (see Chua, 2012; Chua and Iwabuchi, 2008; Kang, 2015; Kim, 2013; Ryoo, 2009; Yoon and Jin, 2017). The Korean wave, which began in the mid-1990s, refers to the global popularity of Korea's cultural economy in exporting pop culture, entertainment, music, TV dramas, and movies. Bong Joon-ho's film *Parasite* won the Palme d'Or in 2019 (Kermode, 2020) and became the first foreign language winner of an Academy Award for Best Picture (Shoard, 2020). There has been growing academic interest in Korean culture since the 2000s. For example, Shim (2006) and Ryoo (2009) contextualised the Korean wave in relation to globalisation and cultural hybridisation. Also, as an indication of such interest, BTS: A Global Interdisciplinary Conference was held at Kingston University, UK, in January 2020. There, various subjects including marketing strategies, transmedia storytelling, gender, performativity, fandom, and Hallyu in relation to the BTS phenomenon were discussed (Kingston University, 2020).

However, it is still not very well known how the Korean wave has been incorporated into branded communications. This book offers an academic immersion in a very dynamic and evolving Korean market and delineates most up-to-date cases. It thus offers fresh and interesting materials for readers who are interested in the Korean media, advertising, marketing, and entertainment industries. It also aims to make a timely contribution to the field by providing a critically informed analysis of those current examples.

Outline of the book

Chapter 1 offers a broad outline of the development of the media and marketing communications industries in Korea and their interrelationship. To contextualise the information, a brief summary of key developments in the Korean media, alongside the key political and social events, is presented.

Chapter 2 discusses branded entertainment, starting from the origin of product placement strategies in movies, to advergames, webtoons, and beyond. Convergence between digital technologies and popular culture makes the boundaries between content and promotion increasingly blurred and hard to distinguish. However, there are continuities as well as changes in these trends. Detailed discussion on the typology of product placement and branded entertainment will be provided in this chapter.

Chapter 3 uses primary research conducted over a two-year period (2018–2019) and consults contemporary research on branded entertainment. Over 30 cases from 2013 to 2019 are used to provide a useful breakdown depending on the format or genre, in order to address one of the biggest challenges in researching branded entertainment, namely, *categorisation*. There are several reasons why it is difficult to establish an exhaustive categorisation or classification system regarding branded entertainment. First, this is due to the increasingly blurred boundaries between promotion and content, which results in a loose definition. Second, the scope of branded entertainment is often unclear as related marketing communications activities such as product placement overlap with branded entertainment. Third, branded entertainment is a constantly evolving discipline, keeping pace with changes in the mediascape and audience. This chapter examines seven categories of branded entertainment – music/music video, web drama, web movie, brand webtoon, web reality show/entertainment show, advergame, and creator contents – and discusses the details of each campaign and relevant issues around conceptual, practical, ethical, and regulatory aspects.

Chapter 4 extends this discussion to examine ethical questions and regulation in the branded entertainment industry in Korea. It addresses a range of critical issues such ethics, regulation, authenticity, creative autonomy, and consumer literacy. Upon the examination of these current examples, I underline the key issues, Defining branded content for the digital age challenges, and prospects of branded entertainment in Korea.

Notes

1 Local loop unbundling (LLU) is a process by which the dominant provider's local loops are physically disconnected from its network and connected to another communications provider's network. This enables competing providers partly or wholly to lease a customer's access line and provide voice and/or data services directly to end users (Ofcom, 2005).

2 Article 73 (Commercial Broadcasts, etc.) (1) A broadcasting business operator shall clearly separate commercial broadcasts from broadcast programmes so as to avoid any confusion, and shall, at the time for commercial broadcasts and for spot commercials before and after a broadcast programme which is oriented to children as its main audience, inscribe captions clarifying it as a commercial without fail under the conditions prescribed by the Presidential Decree so that children may distinguish broadcast programmes from commercial broadcasts. <Amended by Act No. 8060, Oct. 27, 2006>

Bibliography

Appleyard, B. (2010). Advertising is dead, say Lucie Beudet and David Creuzot. *The Sunday Times*. 19 December, pp. 18–19.

BBC (2016). Live from South Korea: the most wired place on earth, BBC World Service, Business Matters, 2 September. Available at www.bbc.co.uk/programmes/p045wgyq

Bhargava, R. (2011). A promising future for branded entertainment. Ogilvy. 15 April. Available at: http://blog.ogilvypr.com/2011/04/a-promising-future-for-branded-entertainment/

Branded Content Marketing Association (BCMA) (2016). BCMA members welcome new definition of branded content. Available at: www.thebcma.info/bcma-members-welcome-new-definition-of-branded-content/

Caraccioli-Davis, L. (2005). Smashing the myths of branded entertainment. *Television Week*. **24**(28), 10–11.

Chae, M-J., and Sun, H-J. (2013). TV product placement in Korea. *Journal of Promotion Management*. **19**(1), 54–75.

Charton, G. (2020). How COVID-19 is impacting the ecommerce market. *The Drum*. 24 March. Available at: www.thedrum.com/opinion/2020/03/24/how-covid-19-impacting-the-ecommerce-market

Chen, T., and Lee, H-M. (2014). Why do we share? The impact of viral videos dramatized to sell. *Journal of Advertising Research*. **54**(3), 292–303.

Choi, D., Bang, H. Wojdynski, B. W., Lee, Y-I., and Keib, K. M. (2018). How brand disclosure timing and brand prominence influence consumer's intention to share branded entertainment content. *Journal of Interactive Marketing*. **42**, 18–31.

Chua, B. H. (2012). *Structure, audience and soft power in East Asian pop culture.* Aberdeen: Hong Kong University Press.

Chua, B. H., and Iwabuchi, K., eds. (2008). *East Asian pop culture: analysing the Korean wave.* Aberdeen: Hong Kong University Press.

Dagnino, G. (2020). *Branded entertainment and cinema: the marketisation of Italian film.* Abingdon: Routledge.

DeMers, J. (2016) Is traditional advertising dead? *Forbes Online.* 22 March. Available at: www.forbes.com/sites/jaysondemers/2016/03/22/is-traditional-advertising-dead/#3dd9377bdb59

Donaton, S. (2004). *Madison & Vine.* New York: McGraw-Hill

Donaton, S. (2007). Madison & Vine: a look back, a look ahead. *AdAge.* 11 October.

Eagle, L., and Dahl, S. (2018). Product placement in old and new media. Journal of Business Ethics. 147(3), 605–618.

Grainge, P. (2011). A song and dance: branded entertainment and mobile promotion. *International Journal of Cultural Studies.* **15**(2), 165–180.

Hardy, J. (2010). *Cross-Media Promotion.* New York: Peter Lang.

Hardy, J. (2012). Comparing media systems. In: F. Esser and T. Hanitzsch, eds. *The handbook of comparative communication research.* New York and Abingdon: Routledge

Hardy, J. (2018). Branded content: media and marketing integration. In: J. Hardy, H. Powell, and I. Macrury, eds. *Advertising handbook.* 4th ed. Abingdon and New York: Routledge, pp. 102–122.

Hudson, S., and Hudson, D. (2006). Branded entertainment: a new advertising technique or product placement in disguise? *Journal of Marketing Management.* **22**(5–6), 489–504.

Hyundai Worldwide (2019a). Calling all fans, lovers of #Hyundai and #BTS. Twitter, 24 May. Available at: https://twitter.com/Hyundai_Global/status/1131838035333718017

Hyundai Worldwide (2019b). What you need to do to win! Twitter, 24 May. Available at: https://twitter.com/Hyundai_Global/status/1131838045785714688

Jeong, Y., and Kim, Y. (2018). A review of Korea-related advertising research. In: D. Y. Jin and N. Kwak, eds. *Communication, digital media, and popular culture in Korea.* Lanham, MD: Lexington Books, chap. 8.

Jin, D-Y. (2013). Hybridization of Korean popular culture: films and online gaming. In: Y. Kim, ed. *The Korean wave: Korean media go global.* Abingdon and New York: Routledge, pp. 148–164.

Kang, I. (2015). The political economy of idols: South Korea's neoliberal restructuring and its impact on the entertainment labour force. In: J-B. Choi and R. Maliangkay, eds. *K-pop: the international rise of the Korean music industry.* New York: Routledge, pp. 51–64.

Kermode, M. (2020). Parasite review – a gasp-inducing masterpiece. *The Guardian.* 10 February. Available at: www.theguardian.com/film/2020/feb/09/parasite-review-bong-joon-ho-tragicomic-masterpiece

Khang, H., Han, S., Shin, S., and Jung, A. R. (2016). A retrospective on the state of international advertising research in advertising, communication, and marketing journals: 1963–2014. *Journal of Advertising.* **35**(3), 540–568.

Kim, Y., ed. (2013). *The Korean wave: Korean media go global.* Abingdon and New York: Routledge.

Kingston University (2020). BTS: A Global Interdisciplinary Conference Project.

Korea Communications Commission (KCC) (2010). Revised contents according to a new revision of broadcasting code enforcement ordinance. 19 January. Korea Communications Commission press release. [in Korean]

Korea Information Society Development Institute (KISDI) (2001). *Evaluation and Issues of the Regulatory Reforms in the Telecommunications Sector of Korea*, December. [in Korean].

Korea Ministry of Government Legislation (2020). *Broadcasting Act.* 9 April. Available at: www.law.go.kr

Kunz, R., Elsässer, F., and Santomier, J. (2016). Sport-related branded entertainment: the Red Bull phenomenon. *Sport, Business and Management: An International Journal.* **6**(5), 520–541.

Lankov, A. (2019). How Korea has become world's most wired country. *The Korea Times.* 7 June. Available at: www.koreatimes.co.kr/www/news/special/2012/05/113_80600.html

Lehu, J-M. (2009). *Branded entertainment.* London: Kogan Page.

Lim, S. (2020). Lazada CMO on why the future of e-commerce is combining livestreaming & entertainment. *The Drum.* 16 April. Available at: www.thedrum.com/news/2020/04/16/lazada-cmo-why-the-future-e-commerce-combining-livestreaming-entertainment

Lotz, A. D. (2007). *The television will be revolutionized.* New York: New York University Press.

Matteo, S., and Zotto, C. D. (2015). Native advertising, or how to stretch editorial to sponsored content within a transmedia branding era. In: G. Siegert, K. Förster, S. M. Chan-Olmsted, and M. Ots, eds. *Handbook of media branding.* Cham, Switzerland: Springer International, pp. 169–185.

McCarthy, T. (2019). We're the bad guy: inside the shocking new film about wild fish. *The Guardian.* 8 May. Available at: www.theguardian.com/film/2019/may/08/artifishal-film-fish-salmon-climate-change

Ministry of Culture, Sports and Tourism (2019). *Advertising Industry Survey 2019. 2019 광고산업조사 2018년 기준*, December. Seoul: Ministry of Culture, Sports and Tourism.

Ministry of Information and Communication (MIC) (2003). *Performance and Task of IT Policy for the last 5 years.* Seoul: Ministry of Information and Communication (MIC). [in Korean]

Ministry of Science and ICT and Korean Broadcast Advertising Corporation (KOBACO) (2018). *방송통신광고비 조사보고서*, December. Seoul: Ministry of Science and ICT and KOBACO.

Office of Communications (Ofcom) (2005). *Local loop unbundling: setting the fully unbundled rental charge ceiling and minor amendment to SMP conditions FA6 and FB6.* 30 November.

O'Guinn, T., Allen, C., and Semenik, R. (2009). *Advertising and integrated brand promotion.* 5th ed. Mason, OH: South-Western Cengage Learning.

Oh, M., and Larson, J. (2011). *Digital development in Korea: building an information society.* Abingdon and New York: Routledge.

Olenski, S. (2016). Branded content, equity content and why brands need to know the difference. *Forbes.* 24 January. Available at: www.forbes.com/sites/steveolenski/2016/06/24/branded-content-equity-content-and-why-brands-need-to-know-the-difference/#18d428f038ed

Picard, R. G., and Russi, L. (2012). Comparing media markets. In: F. Esser and T. Hanitzsch, eds. *The handbook of comparative communication research.* New York and Abingdon: Routledge.

PQ Media (2018). *Global branded entertainment marketing forecast 2018.* Available at: www.pqmedia.com/wp-content/uploads/2018/05/Global-BE-18-15373577.pdf

Raunio, J-M., and Arhio, T. (2015). If you're not at least thinking about branded content, you're missing out. *Adweek.* 30 April. Available at: www.adweek.com/tv-video/if-youre-not-least-thinking-about-branded-content-youre-missing-out-164378/

Russell, C., and Belch, M. (2005). A managerial investigation into the product placement industry. *Journal of Advertising Research.* **45**(1), 73–92.

Ryoo, W. (2009). Globalization, or the logic of cultural hybridization: the case of the Korean wave. *Asian Journal of Communication.* **19**(2), 137–151.

Ryu, C-R, Kim, D-H., and Kim, E-M. (2003). Diffusion of broadband and online advertising in Korea. *Journal of Interactive Advertising.* **4**(1), 3–12.

Shim, D. (2006), Hybridity and the rise of Korean popular culture in Asia. *Media, Culture & Society.* **28**(1), 25–44.

Shin, K. H., and Shin, I. S. (2013). *Advertising in Korea.* 5th ed. Seoul: Communication Books.

Shoard, C. (2020). Parasite makes Oscars history as first foreign language winner of best picture. *The Guardian.* 10 February. Available at: www.theguardian.com/film/2020/feb/10/parasite-first-foreign-language-film-to-win-best-picture-oscar

Spurgeon, C. (2008). *Advertising and new media.* New York: Routledge.

Spurgeon, C. (2015). Regulating integrated advertising. In: M. P. McAllister and E. West, E., eds. *The Routledge companion to advertising and promotional culture.* New York and Abingdon: Routledge, pp. 71–82.

Steinberg, S. R., and Cannella, G. S., eds. (2012). *Critical qualitative research reader.* New York: Peter Lang.

Turow, J. (2016). *Media today: mass communication in a converging world.* 6th ed. New York and London: Routledge.

Tusing, D. (2019). Kriss Kyle on jumping off a chopper with his bike in Dubai. *Gulf News.* 2 February. Available at: https://gulfnews.com/entertainment/hollywood/kriss-kyle-on-jumping-off-a-chopper-with-his-bike-in-dubai-1.61830424

Valero, D. (2014). *Branded entertainment: dealmaking strategies & techniques for industry professionals.* Plantation, FL: J. Ross Publishing.

Van Loggerenberg, M. J. C., Enslin, C., and Terblanche-Smit, M. (2019). Towards a definition for branded entertainment: an exploratory study. *Journal of Marketing Communications*, published online 22 July. Available from doi: 10.1080/13527266.2019.1643395

Van Reijmersdal, E. A., Neijens, P. C., and Smit, E. G. (2007). Effects of television brand placement on brand image. *Psychology & Marketing*. **24**(5), 403–420.

WARC (World Advertising Research Centre) (2020). Global entertainment industry saw record revenues in 2019. News. 13 March. Available at: www.warc.com/newsandopinion/news/globalentertainmentindustrysa wrecordrevenuesin2019/43361?utm_source=daily-email-free-link&utm_ medium=email&utm_campaign=daily-email-emea-prospects-20200313

Woodrooffe, S. (2014). Reimagining branded entertainment: Q&A with CAA Marketing's Jesse Coulter. *Sparksheet*. 28 May. Available at: http://sparksheet. com/reimaginingbranded-entertainment-qa-caa-marketings-jesse-coulter/

Yoon, T-J., and Jin, D. Y. (eds.) (2017). *The Korean Wave: Evolution, Fandom, and Transnationality*. Lanham: Lexington Books.

1 Media and advertising in Korea

Korea has a saturated media market, with media being highly dependent on advertising revenue (Seo, 2020).[1] This chapter will briefly outline the key developments in media and advertising in Korea and then explain three aspects: the Korean wave, internet and mobile communications, and the impact of new forms of digital content on branded entertainment in greater details.

Brief overview

Historically, Korea underwent Japanese colonialism (1910–1945), the arbitrary division by Western powers into opposed states of North and South (1948), the Korean War (1950–1953), and the military rule and successive authoritarian regimes (1961–1993) (Kim, 2013). Despite the movement of democratisation towards a more pluralistic system and press freedom since 1987, there was still the quasi-monopoly of two national TV networks, the Korean Broadcasting System (KBS) and the Munhwa Broadcasting System (MBC), and the oligopoly of three family-run, conservative, national dailies, *Chosun Ilbo*, *JoongAng Ilbo*, and *Dong-Ah Ilbo*, which dominated market share (Lee, 1997; Kim and Johnson, 2009). Table 1.1 summarises the key facts about the development in Korean media and advertising history from the 1880s to 2019.

Currently, there are three public broadcasters (KBS, EBS, and MBC) and one commercial broadcaster, SBS. The Comprehensive Programming Channels, which started in 2011, consist of JTBC, MBN, Channel A, and TV Chosun. In-programme advertising is not permitted on terrestrial channels but is allowed on pay TV channels. Korea's pay TV market has been continuously growing since its inception, but since 2018, the emergence and growing popularity of over-the-top (OTT) services led to declining profits for both IPTV (2.3 per cent decline in 2018 from previous year) and cable TV sector (10.9 per cent decline

Table 1.1 A brief chronology of the media and advertising industry in Korea (1880s to 2019)

Year	Political/mass media development
1880s	The Ganghwa Treaty signed between Korea and Japan in 1876, and Korea opens its doors. In 1880s, Korea signs treaties with Western powers.
1883	First Korean newspaper, *Hanseong Sunbo*, published.
1886	First newspaper advertisement placed in *Hanseong Jubo* by a German trading company.
1896	*Toknip Shinmum* (*The Independent*), the first private bilingual daily, established by Dr. Seo Jae Pil (Philip Jaisohn, a Korean naturalised American). It closed in 1899. A few other dailies and magazines launched.
1904	Ernest T. Bethell, a British citizen, establishes *Daehan Maeil Sinbo* (*Korean Daily*), a bilingual (Korean and English) newspaper.
1905	Korea becomes a Japanese protectorate. Japanese-language dailies start to publish in major cities.
1906	Denpo Tsushinsha (present Dentsu), the Japanese news and advertising agency, establishes its Seoul office.
1907	*Seoul Press*, an English daily, the organisation for the Japanese authority, established.
1910	Japan annexes Korea. Harsh militaristic rule begins. *Daehan Maeil Sinbo*, with '*Daehan* (Great Korea)' stripped from its title, becomes the only Korean-language daily for the colonial government's publicity. Advertising continues. In 1919, the Samil (March 1) Independence Movement breaks out but is suppressed.
1920	Japan switches to a 'Cultural Policy' and two Korean-language dailies, the *Chosun Ilbo* and the *Dong-A Ilbo*, are established. Magazines also start publication.
1927	Kyungsung Radio (JODK; NHK Radio) starts broadcasting in Seoul. No commercials are permitted.
1930s	Japan invades Manchuria in 1931 and China in 1937. National Mobilisation proclaimed. Koreans are forced to change their names to Japanese style.
1940	Two leading Korean-language dailies are forced to close. Only one Korean-language daily remains as the colonial government's publicity organisation.
1945	After World War II, Japanese occupation ends with Soviet troops occupying area north of the 38th parallel, and US troops in the south. Korean dailies resume publication. Korea is divided into North and South along the 38th parallel.
1948	Republic of Korea proclaimed. Dr. Rhee Syngman is elected president.
1950	North Korea invades the South and the Korean War breaks out, lasting for three years.
1953	Armistice ends Korean War, which has cost two million lives. Korea remains divided along the 38th parallel.

Table 1.1   Cont.

Year	Political/mass media development
1950s	South Korea sustained by crucial US military, economic, and political support. In 1953, Christian Broadcasting Station (CBS), the first private radio station, established. No commercials are accepted.
1956	A private TV broadcaster, *Daehan (*KORCAD Television Station), established in 1956 and accepts commercials. It closes in 1959 because of fire.
1956	*Korea Newspaper Annual* published for the first time. Total circulation of 10 national and 20 local dailies: 1,423,800 broken down to 775,800 (54%) morning and 648,000 (46%) evening papers.
1959	MBC, a private radio station, established in Busan. The first Jinro Brewery jingle aired.
1960	President Lee Syngman steps down after student protests against electoral fraud. New constitution forms Second Republic, but political freedom remains limited. An influx of print media follows. The short-lived Chang Myeon administration established.
1961	Military coup puts General Park Chung-hee in power. Tight press control exists. MBC Radio Seoul established.
1963	General Park restores some political freedom and proclaims Third Republic. Major programme of industrial development begins. The government-run KBS accepts commercials to augment its revenue. Discontinues advertising partially after MBC TV is established in 1969.
1964	TBC radio/TV, DBS radio established.
1969	MBC TV established.
1970s	Korean economy grows by leaps and bounds. The Miracle on the Han River. Per-capita GNP reaches $1,600 by 1979 from less than $100 in the early 1960s. Exports hit $10 billion.
1979	Park assassinated. General Chun Doo Hwan seizes power the following year.
1980	General Chun Doo Hwan takes power. Basic Press Law proclaimed and forced mergers of both print and broadcast media effected. Colour TV starts.
1981	The Korea Broadcasting Advertising Corporation (KOBACO), a government agency, established as the exclusive sales representative for broadcast advertising. PC: First computer development starts; computers for educational purposes produced in 1982.
1980s	Increasing shift towards high-tech and computer industry. In 1986, changes in constitution to allow direct election of the president. Analogue mobile communication: Radio paging service starts in 1982. Car telephone service starts in 1984.
1987	President Chun pushed out of office by student unrest and international pressure in the build-up to the Sixth Constitution. General Roh Tae Woo succeeds President Chun, grants greater degree of political liberalisation, and launches anti-corruption drive. Basic Press Law abolished. Number of print and broadcast media shows explosive growth.

(*continued*)

Table 1.1 Cont.

Year	Political/mass media development
1988	Olympic Games in Seoul. First free parliamentary elections. Analogue mobile communication: Mobile communication starts. PC communication: PC communication service starts (*Chollian*)
1991	North and South Korea join the United Nations.
1993	President Roh succeeded by Kim Young Sam, a former opponent of the regime and the first freely elected civilian president.
1994	Kim Il Sung of North Korea dies. Internet: KT's internet service KORNET starts.
1995	Cable TV: Analogue cable TV broadcasting starts
1996	South Korea admitted to Organisation for Economic Co-operation and Development (OECD). Per-capita GNP reaches $11,385. Digital mobile communication: PCS service starts.
1997	Asian financial crisis hits Korea. Internet: Yahoo Korea Portal service starts. Daum's Hanmail service starts.
1998	South Korea is bailed out with $50 billion International Monetary Fund (IMF) emergency rescue fund. Nationwide campaign to rescue Korea from financial crisis spreads. High-speed internet: *Durunet* starts.
1999	Daum café and Naver portal service start. High-speed internet: ADSL service (*Hanaro*) starts.
2002	Korea and Japan co-host the FIFA World Cup. Satellite TV: KT Skylife service starts. High-speed internet: Wireless LAN service starts.
2003	Roh Moo Hyun is elected president. Satellite TV: HDTV service starts.
2005	DMB (Digital Multimedia Broadcasting): Satellite DMB (SK Telecom TU Media) service starts. Terrestrial DMB service starts. Cable TV: Digital cable TV starts.
2007	Digital mobile communication: 3G service starts.
2008	Lee Myung-Bak is elected president. IPTV (Internet Protocol Television): KT IPTV service starts. Smartphone: Samsung Omnia launches.
2009	IPTV: LG U-Plus, SK Broadband IPTV services start. Satellite TV: OTS (Olleh TV Skylife; KT's hybrid broadcast product) service starts. Smartphone: Apple iPhone launches in Korea.
2010	OTT (over-the-top): TV service starts. Tablet PC: Apple iPad launches in Korea. Galaxy Tab launches.
2011	PP (program provider): Comprehensive programming channels start. Digital mobile communication: LTE (4G) service starts.
2012	Digital switchover of the terrestrial TV. OTT: Pooq service starts. DMB: Satellite DMB service finishes.
2013	Park Geun-Hye is elected president.
2014	OTT: *everyon TV* service starts. Cable TV: 8VSB (8-level vestigial sideband; only allowed for terrestrial TV providers in the past) now permitted for cable TV providers.

Table 1.1 Cont.

Year	Political/mass media development
2016	President Park Geun Hye is impeached. OTT: Netflix launches in Korea. Satellite TV: DCS (Dish Convergence Solution) permitted.
2017	Moon Jae-In is elected president. UHD Broadcasting starts for all three terrestrial TV networks (KBS, MBC, and SBS).
2018	Kim Jong Un becomes first North Korean leader to enter the South when he meets President Moon Jae-In for talks at Panmunjom border crossing
2019	OTT: Wavve service starts. Wavve is the combined contents platform between Pooq and SKT's Oksusu. Digital mobile communication: 5G service starts.

Source: Author's table, compiled from 2019 *Broadcasting Industry Report* (Ministry of Science and ICT and Korean Communications Commission, 2019); Shin and Shin (2013: 25–104); BBC (2018) South Korea – Timeline.

from previous year) (Lee, 2019). Korea's paid-for online video market is one of the biggest in Asia, with annual average revenue per user at $97 (approx. £78) for subscription services in 2016, compared to $103 (approx. £83) in Japan and $31 (approx. £25) in China (Cher, 2017). The Korean market is projected to more than triple to $433m (approx. £349m) in 2021 from $142m (approx. £114m) in 2016, according to IHS Markit (Cher, 2017). This is because of 'high smartphone adoption, availability of low-priced subscription services, as well as the entrance of new local and international services' (Cher, 2017).

In terms of advertising regulation, the Korea Communication Commission (KCC) is the statutory regulator and the Korea Advertising Review Board (KARB) undertakes self-regulation. In addition, the Korea Fair Trade Commission (KFTC) assures accuracy in advertising, providing legal guidelines for matters relating to unfair or misleading advertising. There is also the Korea Internet & Security Agency (KISA), which operates the Online Advertising Dispute Mediation Committee in order to deal with the growing number of small disputes in online advertising (Kwon, 2018).

The Korean wave

The Korean wave needs to be understood in the wider context of East Asian popular culture and the Korean government's drive to target the export of popular media culture as a new economic initiative in the 1990s. According to Chua and Iwabuchi (2008: 2–3), the flows and exchanges within the East Asian popular culture sphere have been governed by the disproportionately large ethnic Chinese consumer market relative to those of Japan and Korea, and by differences in domestic economic capacity and the history of the media industries. In addition, memories and other legacies of colonisation and wars have influenced the flows and exchanges of pop cultures within East Asia (Chua and Iwabuchi, 2008: 3). Chua (2012: 15) explains the structural configuration of the relative national positions in East Asian popular culture as follows:

> in spite of a formal ban since the end of the Second World War, Japanese cultural products continued to flow into Korea through different channels and Korean television stations were happy to appropriate ideas and formats from Japanese programmes for their own productions. Importing increased rapidly after 1989, when the ban was lifted. By the end of the 1990s, as Japanese pop culture waned regionally, Korea stepped into the niche and began to export its pop culture into the region, creating what is called the Korean wave. The Japanese and Korean pop cultures, singularly or together, would not have engendered a regional phenomenon were it not for the presence of the ethnic Chinese population as consumers.

The 1997 Asian financial crisis made the Korean government re-examine the process of modernisation. According to Kim (2013: 5), the seemingly sudden rise of the Korean wave is and an amalgamation of the strategic export policy at a time when the Asian media market was growing rapidly, fuelled by the emergence of an affluent urban middle class in Asia and a globalised consumer culture. By the end of the 1990s Japanese pop culture had waned regionally, which created a niche for Korean cultural exports (Chua, 2012). The initial stage of the Korean wave involved the exporting of TV dramas regionally and later, the exports became more diversified, reaching out internationally, with movies, pop music, games, and so forth (Yoon, 2011). In recent years, K-pop has gained an increasingly wider fan base around the world and more studies have looked at various aspects of K-pop. For example, Jung and Shim (2013) examined the dynamics and practices of K-pop consumption and circulation on social media, using a case study of K-pop fandom in Indonesia and the 'Gangnam Style' phenomenon. They argued that online social distribution of K-pop needs to be understood according to two models: the newly emerging, grassroots-driven, bottom-up model and the existing, corporate-led, top-down model. Kang (2015) also investigated the evolution of K-pop in the context of neoliberal globalisation, which brought neoliberal restructuring in Korea's popular music industry since the Asian financial crisis. Kang (2015: 55–57) highlights that K-pop band members are made through a highly rationalised and systematic business practice, and that 'the de-individualisation, or the loss of individual uniqueness, of idol stars is one of the key consequences of hypercommodification and hyperrationalisation'. K-pop's image and reputation have been tarnished by poor working conditions and unfair contracts, worsened by a recent wave of scandals (Campbell and Kim, 2019).

Despite these critiques, the Korean wave has been used as Korea's nation branding strategy (Cha, Rhee, and Chung, 2017; Chung, 2019). An increasing number of IT and game companies in Korea have also capitalised on K-pop stars, aiming to expand their presence in the global market and increase overseas revenue (Jun, 2019). In addition to large investments by Korean conglomerates such as Samsung, LG, and Hyundai in the entertainment industry since the 1900s (Kang, 2015), corporate partnerships have become increasingly common between media or communication agencies and entertainment companies. For example, Naver, Korea's largest portal operator, has joined hands with Big Hit Entertainment (BTS' agency), while SK Telecom, Korea's top mobile carrier, signed an agreement with SM Entertainment for next-generation media business (Jun, 2019). Overall, since the financial crisis in the late 1990s, Korean government policy initiatives have focused on the public promotion of cultural exports. The digital content sector was not an exception, which will be articulated in the next two sections.

Internet and mobile communications

Competition has been a key driver of mobile diffusion in many countries (Gruber and Verboven, 2001) and Korea is no exception. Korea Mobile Telecom (KMT), the first mobile company owned by the Korean government, started an analogue mobile service in metropolitan areas of Korea in 1984 (Kim, Heo, and Chan-Olmstead, 2010). In 1995, KMT was privatised, with SK Telecom as a main shareholder. Four more companies – LG Telecom, Shinsegi Telecom, KT Freetel (KTF), and Hansol Telecom – entered the mobile market in 1997 (Kim, Heo, and Chan-Olmstead, 2010). Due to the high level of market competition among these companies, the penetration of mobile phones in Korea grew exponentially (Kim, Heo, and Chan-Olmstead, 2010). Currently, the telecommunications and the internet service providers (ISP) markets are dominated by the incumbent KT, as well as by SK and LG (Kim and Kim, 2016).

From the 2000s, a major transformation took place in the Korean media industries, with the rapid growth of internet media and mobile communications. Korea was the first country to introduce mobile television broadcasting through both terrestrial and satellite systems on a large-scale basis (Chan-Olmsted, Lee, and Heo, 2008). In addition, the world's first citizen-based online newspaper, *OhmyNews* (www.ohmynews.com), was founded in 2000 (Kim and Johnson, 2009). A 2004 survey revealed that alongside the top five legacy media (KBS, MBC, *Chosun Ilbo*, *JoongAng Ilbo*, and *Dong-Ah Ilbo*) listed above, three online news media – *OhmyNews*, *PRESSian* (www.pressian.com), and *Media Daum* (www.daum.net) –entered the top ten media outlets for the first time (*Sisa-Journal*, 2004).

The everyday life of Koreans became increasingly tied to mobile devices and, by 2014, the level of smartphone penetration had overtaken that of PCs in the country (Lee 2014). Due to the popularisation of smartphones and high-speed data packages, new forms of digital content started to be developed by industry professionals for audiences to consume on mobile devices, for example, web dramas and webtoons (Kang, 2017). More recently, Reuters reported that Korea launched the world's first commercial 5G service in Seoul in April 2019 (Li and Park, 2019). As the fifth-generation of mobile internet connectivity, 5G allows users to get more data with less delay, wider coverage, and more stable connections (Harrison, 2019). It brought about higher-quality streaming and the ability to livestream to bigger audiences and to provide better experiences for people watching live sports or cloud gaming (Harrison, 2019), and this is a significant development in terms of people's consumption of branded entertainment, especially in the format of webtoons and web dramas, most of which are consumed on mobile devices. This shift in distribution also opened up spaces for less frequently seen content on Korean TV, for example, vampires and aliens (Kang, 2017).

New forms of digital content and its impact on branded entertainment

According to Horloyd (2019), Korea is a powerhouse in both digital hardware and certain digital content sectors like video games and animation, and the strength of the country's digital content sector is rooted in the global popularity of Korean entertainment. The Ministry of Culture, Sports and Tourism established the Korea Creative Content Agency (KOCCA) in 2009. KOCCA brings together five existing organisations: the Korean Broadcasting Institute, the Korea Culture and Content Agency, the Korea Game Development and Promotion

Institute, the Culture and Contents Centre, and the Digital Contents Business Group of the Korea SW Industry Promotion Agency. KOCCA supports the country's creative industries including gaming, animation and characters, cartoons and comics, music, broadcasting, fashion for local content production, expansion overseas, investment attraction, and the development and training of creative talent (Horloyd, 2019).

In the digital content sector, three key areas of growth in branded entertainment are games, webtoons, and web dramas. Firstly, Korea has capitalised on the country's highly successful online gaming industry (Horloyd, 2019). Revenue from Korea's gaming sector alone was slightly under US$2.2 billion in 2017, with a projected annual growth rate of 6.3 per cent (United Nations Conference on Trade and Development, 2017). Secondly, the popularity of webtoons has also grown steadily since the mid-2000s (Kim and Yu, 2019: 1) and the KOCCA reported that webtoons accounted for more than 70 per cent of the domestic comic market, which was estimated at around $894 million in 2017 (Baek, 2018). However, the issue of exploitation of labour, among others, has been raised in recent years, questioning webtoon production and the relationship between platform and labour (Kim and Yu, 2019). 'Platformisation' is an important concept to understand the Korean webtoon industry. Poell, Nieborg, and van Dijck (2019: 1) define platformisation as 'the penetration of infrastructures, economic and governmental frameworks of digital platforms in different economic sectors and spheres of life, as well as the reorganisation of cultural practices and imaginations around these platforms'. The power relations among platform operators, end users, and complementors are extremely volatile and inherently asymmetrical as operators are fully in charge of a platform's techno-economic development (Poell, Nieborg, and van Dijck, 2019). As all webtoons in Korea these days are published on centralised platforms such as Naver and Daum through an open and laissez-faire contest, many cartoonists desperate for exposure work hard but are poorly compensated. This is where branded entertainment comes in. The problem of an insufficient revenue policy of the existing platforms for these content producers led them to rely on product placement and branded entertainment (Kang, 2017).

Thirdly, another digital content, web drama, has also often been used as branded entertainment. Coupled with the needs of the web drama industry to find a sustainable revenue model, the branded entertainment strategy has become noticeable in many web dramas (Kang, 2017). Web dramas do not have any regulations in place yet, but recent developments in the Korea Fair Trade Commission's dealing with unethical practices of brands and micro-influencers (see Chapter 3) indicate that this will change soon. Jin (2020) uses the concept of 'snack culture' to explain why webtoons and web dramas are widely consumed on mobiles in Korea. First coined by *Wired* in 2007, snack culture explains a modern tendency to look for a convenient culture that is indulged within a short duration of time, depicting the changing habit of cultural consumption (Jin, 2020). With this trend of snack culture, superfast broadband services and widely available smartphones enable people to watch webtoons and web dramas on the go. It is for this reason that marketers seek to use these formats.

Since its genesis in the 1990s, K-pop has matured to a $5 billion (approximately £4 billion) industry (Sinha, 2018). This has had an overall positive impact on the promotion of various brands (some of which campaigns are covered in Chapter 3), including the nation itself. The advertising industry grew in size and also became more sophisticated over time. According to Cheil Worldwide, advertising spending in Korea grew 2.3 per cent to $10.05 billion in 2019, with digital spend surpassing $4.2 billion in 2019, capturing 42.2 per cent of total spend and mobile growing by 17.2 per cent (Campaign Asia-Pacific, 2020). Ongoing diversification of platforms and rapid growth in digital spend are also worth our attention. Digital spend is expected to surpass traditional media for the first time in 2020 (Campaign Asia-Pacific, 2020).

In conclusion, Korea has a dynamic media environment with diverse content providers, ranging from terrestrial, cable, and satellite broadcasters, telecommunication providers, and mobile companies, to OTT service providers. Since the 1990s, Korea has experienced several distinctive changes in politics, economy, and technology, which are directly related to the development of local media and culture (Jin and Kwak, 2018: xiii). These political, economic, and sociocultural factors help explain the context in which branded entertainment has developed to operate. The next chapter will elaborate on the origins, definitions, issues, and challenges in the theory and practice of branded entertainment.

Note

1 Seo (2020) identifies Korea as somewhere between the polarised pluralist and liberal systems in reference to the models of Western media systems advanced by Hallin and Mancini (2004, 2012).

Bibliography

Baek, B-Y. (2018). Webtoon makers leaving Korea for US, Japan. *Korea* Times. 1 August. Available at: www.koreatimes.co.kr/www/tech/2018/08/133_253135.html

BBC (2018). South Korea – Timeline. Available at: www.bbc.co.uk/news/world-asia-pacific-15292674

Campaign Asia-Pacific (2020). South Korea ad market to hit US$10.6 billion this year: Cheil. 20 February. Available at: www.campaignasia.com/article/south-korea-ad-market-to-hit-us10-6-billion-this-year-cheil/458274

Campbell, M., and Kim, S. (2019). The dark side of K-Pop: assault, prostitution, suicide, and spycams. *Bloomberg Businessweek*, 6 November. Available at: www.bloomberg.com/news/features/2019-11-06/k-pop-s-dark-side-assault-prostitution-suicide-and-spycams

Cha, H., Rhee, Y., and Chung, C-J. (2017). Comparative nation-branding analysis of Big Data: focusing on Korea and Japan. *Journal of Global Information Technology Management*, **20**(4), 276–295.

Chan-Olmsted, S. M., Lee, S., and Heo, J. (2008). Developing a mobile television market: lessons from the world's leading mobile economy – South Korea. *Proceedings of the 8th World Media Economics Conference*. Lisbon, Portugal.

Cher, B. (2017). South Korea's paid-for video market to triple by 2021. The Drum, 8 June, www.thedrum.com/news/2017/06/08/south-korea-s-paid-video-market-triple-2021

Chua, B. H. (2012). *Structure, audience and soft power in East Asian pop culture*. Aberdeen: Hong Kong University Press.

Chua, B. H., and Iwabuchi, K. (eds) (2008). *East Asian pop culture: analysing the Korean wave*. Aberdeen: Hong Kong University Press.

Chung, K-Y. (2019). Media as soft power: the role of the South Korean media in North Korea. *The Journal of International Communication*, **25**(1), 137–157.

Gruber, H., and Verboven, F. (2001). The evolution of markets under entry and standards regulation: the case of global mobile telecommunications. *International Journal of Industrial Organization*, **19**, 1189–1212.

Hallin, D., and Mancini, P. (2004). *Comparing media systems: three models of media and politics*. New York: Cambridge University Press.

Hallin, D., and Mancini, P. (2012). *Comparing media systems beyond the Western world*. New York: Cambridge University Press.

Harrison, V. (2019). 5G: world's first commercial services promise 'great leap'. BBC. 5 April. Available at: www.bbc.co.uk/news/business-47796528

Jin, D-Y. (2020). *Transmedia storytelling in East Asia: the age of digital media*. Abingdon and New York: Routledge.

Jin, D-Y., and Kwak, N. (2018). *Communication, digital media, and popular culture in Korea*. Lanham, MD: Lexington Books.

Jun, J-H. (2019). IT firms target overseas markets with K-pop stars. *Korea Times*. 22 January, www.koreatimes.co.kr/www/tech/2020/02/133_262482.html

Jung, S., and Shim, D. (2013). Social distribution: K-Pop fan practices in Indonesia and the 'Gangnam Style' phenomenon. *International Journal of Cultural Studies*, **17**(5), 485–501.

Kang, I. (2015). The political economy of idols: South Korea's neoliberal restructuring and its impact on the entertainment labour force. In: J-B Choi and R. Maliangkay, eds. *K-pop: the international rise of the Korean music industry*. New York: Routledge, pp. 51–64.

Kang, J. M. (2017). Just another platform for television? The emerging web dramas as digital culture in South Korea, *Media, Culture & Society*, **39**(5), 762–772.

Kim, D., and Johnson, T. J. (2009). A shift in media credibility: comparing internet and traditional news sources in South Korea *International Communication Gazette*. 71(4), 283–302.

Kim, D., and Kim, S-C. (2016). Media ownership and concentration in South Korea. In: E. M. Noam and the International Media Concentration Collaboration, eds. *Who Owns the World's Media?* New York: Oxford University Press, chap. 27.

Kim, J-H., and Yu, J. (2019). Platformizing webtoons: the impact on creative and digital labor in South Korea. *Social Media + Society*. October–December, 1–11.

Kim, M., Heo, J., and Chan-Olmsted, S. M. (2010). Perceived effectiveness and business structure among advertising agencies: a case study of mobile advertising in South Korea. *Journal of Media Business Studies*. 7(2), 1–20.

Kim, Y. (ed.) (2013). *The Korean wave: Korean media go global*. Abingdon, Oxon: Routledge.

Korea Broadcast Advertising Corporation (KOBACO) (2020). Introduction. Available at: www.kobaco.co.kr/site/eng/content/introduction

Korea Communications Commission (KCC) (2020). About KCC, Overview. Available at: https://eng.kcc.go.kr/user.do?page=E01010100&dc=E01010100#none

Kwon, Y-K. (2018). 온라인 광고 관련 경쟁법 이슈와 시사점, *Korea Fair Trade Mediation Agency* 한국공정거래조정원,공정거래 이슈브리핑, 3.

Lee, J. (1997). Press freedom and democratization: South Korean's experience and some lessons. *Gazette*. 59(2), 135–149.

Lee, K-T. (2019). 유료방송 빅뱅기, 케이블TV업계 생존 위한 과제는? *Chosun Biz*. 13 October. Available at: https://biz.chosun.com/site/data/html_dir/2019/10/12/2019101201366.html

Lee, M-J. (2014). Smartphone usage overtakes PCs in South Korea. *The Wall Street Journal*. 12 December. Available at: https://blogs.wsj.com/korearealtime/2014/12/12/smartphone-usage-overtakes-pcs-in-south-korea/

Li, K., and Park, J-M. (2019). What was first to launch 5G? Depends who you ask. *Reuters*. 5 April. Available at: www.reuters.com/article/us-telecoms-5g/who-was-first-to-launch-5g-depends-who-you-ask-idUSKCN1RH1V1

Poell, T., Nieborg, D., and van Dijck, J. (2019). Platformisation. *Internet Policy Review. 8*(4), 1–13.

Ryoo, W. (2009). Globalization, or the logic of cultural hybridization: the case of the Korean wave. *Asian Journal of Communication*. 19(2), 137–151.

Seo, S. (2020). South Korea's Watergate Moment: How a Media Coalition Brought Down the Park Geun-hye Government. *Journalism Practice*, published online 21 Feb 2020. Available from https://doi.org/10.1080/17512786.2020.1730221" 10.1080/17512786.2020.1730221

Shin, K. H., and Shin, I. S. (2013). *Advertising in Korea.* 5th ed. Seoul: Communication Books.

Sinha, K. (2018). Asian youth in 2019; K-pop, wellness, sustainability and Bollywood goes to China. *Admap.* December.

Sisa-Journal (2004). 2004 survey: who are moving Korea? Available at: www.sisapress.com

United Nations Conference on Trade and Development (2017). Strengthening the creative industries for development in the Republic of Korea. 24–2017. Available at: http://unctad.org/en/PublicationsLibrary/ditcted2017d4_en.pdf

Yoon, H. (2011). *Mapping out the K-pop fandom in the UK.* New Korean Wave: Asia and Beyond, Asia Pop Culture Forum, 2 September, Seoul.

Yoon, H. (2012). 영국내 한류 현황 및 관련 연구 동향. Yu, S., Hong, S., Yoon, H., Jeong, S., Jeong, J., and Jang, D. *해외 언론의 한류보도 분석 연구.* Seoul: Korea Press Foundation.

2 Branded entertainment
Literature review

The historical context

> In many ways, branded entertainment today has metamorphosed from a discipline born of fear – the fear that audiences empowered by digital technologies would avoid advertising, and that therefore it should be hidden inside a tastier product, sort of like that spoonful of sugar that helps the medicine down – to a more confident and more creative position, this one based on the concept that consumers will accept good content from any source so long as it is transparent, entertaining or informative, and relevant.
>
> (Donaton, 2007)

The current marketing environment is characterised by 'the fragmentation' of audiences, 'media overflow', and 'information overload' (Kunz, Elsässer, and Santomier, 2016: 521). Marketers are therefore challenged to think beyond traditional advertising strategies and this is what constitutes 'the fear' Donaton (2007) talks about in the above quotation. In order to understand how and why this fear came about, this section will consider the historical context of branded entertainment, starting with the evolution of product placement.

Product placement is not a new phenomenon, and the origins of it go back to more than a hundred years ago (Kretchmer, 2004; Turner, 2004; Hudson and Hudson, 2006; Lehu, 2009). Certain films made by Auguste and Louis Lumière in 1896, at the request of François-Henri Lavanchy-Clarke, representative of Lever Brothers in France, represent the first cases of product placement on record (Lehu, 2009: 19–20). Product placement acquired an ongoing business rationale with Thomas Edison's cooperative arrangements with railroads in 1897, and then developed in span and sophistication with the widespread use of tie-ups from the 1920s onwards (Newell, Salmon, and Chang, 2006: 590).

From the 1930s onwards, film producers and brand owners actively engaged in product placement deals (Hudson and Hudson, 2006: 490). In the United States, radio developed as a promotional medium, with the first advertisement in 1922, and by 1929 more than half of the programmes on radio were not only paid for by advertisers but also created by advertisers and ad agencies (Turner, 2004). For example, by the 1930s the J. Walter Thomson Company, one of the largest and most active agencies at the time was producing more than 33 programmes, representing a total of 60 hours of airtime per week (Kretchmer, 2004). In the broadcast media content in the United States, the sponsor's name was often used in the title of programmes: for instance, the *Maxwell House Hour*, *General Motors Family Party*, and *Colgate Comedy Hour* (Kretchmer, 2004).

From the early 1930s until the 1980s, barter-style arrangements were in operation, whereby the brand owner would provide free props to the production set and often lend advertising support to promote the film (Hudson and Hudson, 2006). With the emergence of specialist product placement agencies in the mid-1980s, this relationship started to change (Hudson and Hudson, 2006). As a result, the brand owner benefits from brand exposure and movie makers receive financial support. The term 'product placement' did not come into scholarly or trade use until the 1980s and prior to this point, product placement was referred to as 'exploitation, publicity by motion picture, moving picture advertising, co-operative advertising, trade-outs, tie-ups or tie-ins' (Newell, Salmon, and Chang, 2006).

While there is nothing new about the integration of advertising and media content, commentators are right to emphasise the increasing use of product placement in films from the early 1980s (Lehu, 2009; Hardy, 2010: 234). The film *E.T. the Extra-Terrestrial* (1982) provides an important turning point. The success of the product placement of Reese's Pieces in *E.T.* can be viewed as a typical product placement arrangement that delivered atypical results (Newell, Salmon, and Chang, 2006). No payment was made by the candy manufacturer Hershey's to Universal Pictures, and the producers did not pay Hershey's for the right to use a trademarked item. Instead, all parties shared in the benefits of the tie-up. Potential *E.T.* ticket buyers saw off-screen promotions paid for by Hershey's, and viewers were exposed to the on-screen use of the product. Hershey's saw a 65 per cent rise in sales following the film's release, and ever since, the placement of products in movies and television has become an important element of consumer marketing programmes and has seen considerable growth (Hudson and Hudson, 2006).

To focus specifically on branded entertainment, we can find its origin in the 'soap opera' (Russell, 2007; Lehu, 2009; Van Loggerenberg, Enslin, and Terblanche-Smit, 2019). In the United States, radio shows in the 1930s and later television shows in the 1950s were sponsored by a specific brand, typically soap manufacturers, and this is where the term 'soap opera' came from. Wharton (2015: 42) states that in the United States, the radio brought together the potential to combine commercial activity with entertainment and information in new ways. In the mid-1980s, branded entertainment became more prominent, with a successful case like *E. T.* As discussed in the introduction to this book, branded entertainment holds varied meanings and there are three different takes on it; first, branded entertainment as product placement and integration; second, branded entertainment not as product placement or integration but as brand-generated content with full ownership and control of intellectual property; and lastly, an all-encompassing view such as brand-generated and/or integration with partial control and ownership. Over the years, the definitions of branded entertainment have become a lot more than just a 'placement' of products in movies or television; hence, the notion of 'integration' is given more importance. The next section discusses the ways in which academics and practitioners have conceptualised branded entertainment.

Conceptualising branded entertainment

Media and advertising integration is by no means a new phenomenon and has a long history across all media forms (Hardy, 2013: 147). Product placement, branded entertainment, advergames, and informercials are among the most familiar outcomes (Lehu, 2009; Hardy, 2015: 79). Hardy (2013, 2015) describes this emergent relationship between media and advertising as one of *integration without separation* which coexists with trends towards *disaggregation* of media and advertising. Both trends reflect a new shift towards marketer power in an era of increased competition for advertising finance (Hardy, 2013: 80).

Among the first to provide a conceptual model and a definition for branded entertainment is Hudson and Hudson (2006). They consider branded entertainment as a type of integrated product placement, illustrating the convergence between advertising and entertainment (Hudson and Hudson, 2006: 491). Here, branded entertainment is defined as the integration of advertising into entertainment content, whereby brands are embedded into storylines of a film, television programme, or other entertainment medium, involving co-creation and collaboration between entertainment, media, and brands (Hudson and Hudson, 2006: 492).

Lehu (2009) provides a comprehensive account of branded entertainment, focusing on the evolution of product placement via US examples for the most part and some European examples. Not only did he examine the history and development of product placement, but he also provided practical recommendations and insights. This was, however, more representative of an affirmative perspective, evidenced in his statement that product placement is 'a technique accepted by the audience' (Lehu, 2009: 64). Previously, in *Handbook of Product Placement in the Mass Media* (Galician, 2004), many scholars presented more discursive accounts of the theory and practice of product placement, acknowledging complexity in this growing marketing discipline. For example, Wenner (2004: 128) pointed to product placements in media entertainment as a complex and far-reaching ethical problem as placements and other cross-marketing practices might not be identifiable as advertising to consumers.

The focus of much advertising research from a marketing and business perspective is on assessing marketing communications effectiveness. Such research is affirmative in that it largely accepts and supports existing conditions and follows the research needs and agendas of marketers. The focus in these affirmative studies is *on the effectiveness in relation to a specific aspect of product placement or branded entertainment*. For instance, many researchers focus on how various factors (i.e. memory, recall, brand familiarity, perception, and exposure) relate to the effectiveness of branded entertainment.[1] Findings are mixed even among the studies dealing with the same format: for example, Cauberghe and De Pelsmacker (2010) show no correlation between brand evaluation and exposure to product placements in games, while others such as Mackay et al. (2009) and Mallinckrodt and Mizerski (2007) find product preferences are enhanced by product placements in advergaming.

On the other hand, more critical scholarship on this topic focus on the assessment of issues such as privacy, ethics, regulation, autonomy, literacy, consumer awareness, and acceptance.[2] Such critiques raise questions around problems of media and marketing integration for user, media, and society alike. Einstein (2016: 2) argues that the key aspect of branded entertainment is to engage consumers without their realising they have taken part in a promotional initiative. She calls this 'black ops advertising', a purposeful masking of corporate bias by either advertisers or publishers, which creates 'content confusion' for consumers (Einstein, 2016: 7). Content confusion is the state of uncertainty that occurs when advertising does not look like advertising, making it difficult or impossible to separate media content from advertising. Einstein uses the Red Bull Stratos project to explain this concept.

The Red Bull Stratos project (2012) was a project in which an Austrian skydiver, Felix Baumgartner, became the first human to break the sound barrier without engine power during his jump from high-altitude space to earth (Ogborn, 2019). The live broadcast on YouTube of this jump reached more than eight million viewers (Mortimer, 2012). This event was filmed by an action camera tech company, GoPro, which later formalised their global partnership with Red Bull, spanning content production, cross-promotion, and product innovation (Stewart, 2016). Red Bull's Media House produced TV shows for its Red Bull TV channel and licenced to the Discovery channel, Netflix, and others, while Stratos also secured worldwide publicity in news coverage as 'earned' media (Hardy, 2018: 102). Here, commercial content ambiguously presented in various media platforms led to content confusion. In a recent study on branded entertainment, Dagnino (2020) examined the increasingly central role that advertising and advertisers' interests have been playing in the Italian film industry. Although there are many attempts to conceptualise branded entertainment and to examine the effects of blurred lines between promotion and content on the audience, such as content confusion, research outputs in non-English publications are less accessible. So, the next section considers recent studies in branded entertainment-related topics, published in Korean academic journals. It also examines how product placement and branded entertainment are defined in Korean law.

Literature on branded entertainment in Korea

While there is no legislation or regulation in Korea which mentions the term 'branded entertainment', product placement is defined by the *Broadcasting Act* (Article 73-2) as 'commercials that exposes products, trademarks, names or logos of companies or services and others within broadcast programmes' (Korea Ministry of Government Legislation, 2020). The revised *Broadcasting Act* was approved in January 2010 to allow product placement in terrestrial broadcasting and cable channels in Korea (Chae and Sun, 2013: 67). Under current enforcement ordinance of the *Broadcasting Act* (Article 47), product names and commercial messages of the product should be specifically exposed and mentioned through subtitles, audio, or props (Korea Communications Standards Commission, 2019). It is not permitted to have 'advertising phrases, sounds or images reminiscent of product placements or describing features and advantages' (Article 47).

In recent years, there has been growing interest in branded entertainment or related topics such as branded content, native advertising, and product placement. Some studies were published in Western academic journals (e.g. Chae and Sun, 2013; Kang, 2017; An, Kerr, and Jin 2019), but most of them were published in Korean journals.[3] For example, Chae and Sun (2013) examine product placement in Korean television, while Kang (2017) explores the ways in which distribution on online platforms has influenced the recent development of web dramas in Korea. More recently, An, Kerr, and Jin (2019) have investigated consumers' recognition of in-feed native advertising appearing as news content and found that consumers engaged less with the message, showed less positive attitudes towards the brand, and were less likely to purchase and share the message.

As for the branded entertainment-related research in Korean academia, some studies focus on the characteristics of a particular format of branded entertainment (e.g. ad movies and webtoons) or consumer responses to them. Others are concerned with applying a theoretical framework to the ways in which branded entertainment engages consumers. Less research has been done in the areas of regulatory environment and policy. For example, Hwang and Jeong (2014) examine the persuasive effects of an ad movie, with a special reference to the role played by narrative transportation in the effects of an ad movie and how they vary depending on the exposure to a relevant ad. The participants who are exposed to the ad first, then show less favourable attitudes towards the movie and the brand, but the negative effects of prior exposure to the ad on attitudes are mediated by narrative transportation. In addition to ad movies, webtoons were also analysed. Lee and Hwang (2017) examine the characteristics of 50 webtoons from 2012 to 2017 in terms of their structures and contents. While they find a range of subjects, publication types (such as episode, story, and omnibus), and genres, the most frequently used genre is comedy and the favoured story types are those written by a single author as this allows readers to engage with an ongoing narrative and characters. Brand messages in webtoons account for approximately 20 per cent and, importantly, an excessive brand message turns out to play a negative role in consumer responses.

The theoretical frameworks and conceptual models developed in the West are also applied to Korean examples. Jun (2016) investigates the uses and gratifications of branded entertainment, using a model of content playfulness and value perceptions. User motivations of branded entertainment are time-killing, relaxation/entertainment, and information. Furthermore, time-killing and relaxation/entertainment influence playfulness positively, but time-killing influences content values negatively. In a similar vein, Hong and Jun (2017) show that content novelty and creator attractiveness (social, physical, and professional attractiveness) of branded entertainment on a multi-channel network (MCN) influence purchase intention and sharing intention to a great extent. There is, however, a tendency for the extant research to be heavily reliant on the body of knowledge advanced in a non-Korean or non-Asian context. Each country has a different regulatory environment and media system, and no theory or model comes in a 'one-size-fits-all' form. Thus, more effort is needed in reflecting on the applicability of a theory or model and in identifying areas for modification if needed.

Historically, entertainment and advertising have been inextricably intertwined due to their symbiotic relationship. In recent years, the growth of the entertainment industry and the changes in how entertainment is distributed and consumed have opened the door to integrated advertising, with marketers realising that communications via product placement and branded entertainment can be an effective part of the promotional mix (Hudson and Hudson, 2006). Branded entertainment was recognised by the industry as a distinctive discipline when the Cannes Festival of Creativity created a category of branded entertainment in 2012 (Van Loggerenberg, Enslin, and Terblanche-Smit, 2019). It continued to grow, and in 2017, global branded entertainment marketing revenues rose by 8 per cent to $106.2 billion (approximately £86 billion) (PQ Media, 2018). In 2019, the global entertainment market surpassed $100 billion (approximately £81 billion) in revenues for the first time (WARC, 2020). While the extant research acknowledges the difficulty and complexity of defining branded entertainment and measuring the results, many case studies demonstrate it has clearly attracted significant attention from marketers, publishers, scholars, and consumers alike.

Notes

1 Selected examples of these studies are Avery and Ferraro (2000), Cauberghe and De Pelsmacker (2010), D'Astous and Chartier (2000), Gould and Gupta (2006), Mackay et al. (2009), Mallinckrodt and Mizerski (2007), Morton and Friedman (2002), Nelson (2002), Nelson, Keum, and Yaros (2004), Russell (2002), and Russell and Stern (2006).
2 Selected examples of such studies are Dagnino (2020), Einstein (2016), Galician (2004), Hardy (2010, 2015, 2018), and Turow (2011).
3 Selected examples of those published in Korean are Hwang and Jeong (2014), Han and Moon (2015), Lee and Hwang (2017), Jun (2016), Hong and Jun (2017), Yu and Kim (2018), Park and Yu (2019), and Kang and Jeon (2019).

Bibliography

An, S., Kerr, G., and Jin, H. S. (2019). Recognizing native ads as advertising: attitudinal and behavioral consequences. *Journal of Consumer Affairs.* Winter **53**(4), 1421–1442.

Asmussen, B., Wider, S., Williams, R., Stevenson, N., Whitehead, E., and Canter, A. (2016). *Defining branded content for the digital age. The industry experts' views on branded content as a new marketing communications concept.* A collaborative research project commissioned by the BCMA and conducted by Oxford Brookes University and Ipsos MORI. June.

Avery, R. J., and Ferraro, R. (2000). Verisimilitude or advertising? Brand appearances on prime time television. *Journal of Consumer Affairs.* **34**(2), 217–244.

Cauberghe, V., and De Pelsmacker, P. (2010). Advergames: the impact of brand prominence and game repetition on brand response. *Journal of Advertising.* **39**(1), 5–18.

Chae, M-J., and Sun, H-J. (2013). TV product placement in Korea. *Journal of Promotion Management.* **19**, 54–75.

Dagnino, G. (2020). *Branded entertainment and cinema: the marketisation of Italian film.* London and New York: Routledge.

D'Astous, A., and Chartier, F. (2000). A study of factors affecting consumer evaluations and memory of product placements in movies. *Journal of Current Issues & Research in Advertising.* **22**(2), 31–40.

Donaton, S. (2007). Madison & Vine: a look back, a look ahead. *AdAge.* 11 October.

Einstein, M. (2016). *Black ops advertising: native ads, content marketing, and the covert world of the digital sell.* New York and London: OR Books.

Galician, M-L. (ed) (2004). *Handbook of product placement in the mass media.* New York: Hayworth Press.

Gould, S. J., and Gupta, P. B. (2006). Come on down. *Journal of Advertising.* 35(1), 65–81.

Han, K-H., and Moon, J-H. (2015). '국내 간접광고 규제의 개선방향에 관한 고찰: 해외의 간접광고 규제 사례 분석을 토대로', 광고연구, Spring, 104: 109–146.

Hardy, J. (2010). *Cross-media promotion.* New York: Peter Lang.

Hardy, J. (2013). The changing relationship between media and advertising. In: H. Powell, ed. *Promotional culture and convergence: markets, methods, media.* Abingdon and New York: Routledge, pp. 125–150.

Hardy, J. (2015). Political economy approaches to advertising. In: C. Wharton, ed. *Advertising: critical approaches.* Abingdon, Oxon and New York: Routledge, pp. 65–84.

Hardy, J. (2018). Branded content: media and marketing integration. In: J. Hardy, H. Powell, and I. Macrury, eds. *Advertising handbook*, 4th ed. Abingdon and New York: Routledge, pp. 102–122.

Hong, D., and Jun, J. W. (2017). Effects of MCN branded entertainment on consumer evaluations. *Journal of Public Relations.* **21**(4), 30–55.

36 *Branded entertainment: literature review*

Hudson, S., and Hudson, D. (2006). Branded entertainment: a new advertising technique or product placement in disguise. *Journal of Marketing Management.* **22**(5/6), 489–504.

Hwang, Y., and Jeong, S-H. (2014). Persuasive effects of branded entertainment: focusing on the effects of ad movies. *The Korean Journal of Advertising* 광고학 연구. **25**(6), 83–104.

Jun, J-W. (2016). Effects of uses and gratifications on playfulness and values of branded entertainment content. *Journal of Public Relations.* **20**(5), 1–21.

Kang, J. M. (2017). Just another platform for television? The emerging web dramas as digital culture in South Korea. *Media, Culture & Society.* **39**(5), 762–772.

Kang, J-M., and Jeon, S-M. (2019). Every company is a media company. 커뮤니케이션 이론 *Communication Theory.* **15**(1), 5–56.

Korea Ministry of Government Legislation (2020). *Broadcasting Act.* 9 April. Available at: www.law.go.kr

Korea Communications Standards Commission (2019). 방송심의에 관한 규정. 27 September. 국가법령정보센터.

Kretchmer, S. B. (2004). Advertainment: the evolution of product placement as a mass media marketing strategy. *Journal of Promotion Management.* **10**(1/2), 37–54.

Kunz, R. E., Elsässer, F., and Santomier, J. (2016). Sport-related branded entertainment: the Red Bull phenomenon. *Sport, Business and Management.* **6**(5), 520–541.

Lee, J., and Hwang, J-S. (2017). Characteristics of and consumers' responses to brand webtoons. 광고연구 *Advertising Research.* Winter, 115, 246–296.

Lehu, J-M. (2009). *Branded entertainment.* London: Kogan Page.

Mackay, T., Ewing, M., Newton, F., and Windisch, L. (2009). The effect of product placement in computer games on brand attitude and recall. *International Journal of Advertising.* **28**(3), 423–438.

Mallinckrodt, V., and Mizerski, D. (2007). The effects of playing an advergame on young children's perceptions, preferences, and requests. *Journal of Advertising.* **36**(2), 87–100.

Mortimer, R. (2012). Red Bull flies to another level with marketing wins. *Marketing Week.* 17 October. Available at: www.marketingweek.com/red-bull-flies-to-another-level-with-marketing-wins/

Morton, C. R., and Friedman, M. (2002). 'I saw it in the movies': exploring the link between product placement beliefs and reported usage behavior. *Journal of Current Issues & Research in Advertising.* **24**(2), 33–40.

Nelson, M. R. (2002). Recall of brand placements in computer/video games. *Journal of Advertising Research.* **42**(2), 80–92.

Nelson, M. R., Keum, H., and Yaros, R. A. (2004), Advertisement or adcreep? Game players' attitudes toward advertising and product placements in computer games. *Journal of Interactive Advertising.* **4**(3), 3–21.

Newell, J. Salmon, C. T., and Chang, S. (2006). The hidden history of product placement. *Journal of Broadcasting & Electronic Media.* **50**(4), 575–594.

Ogborn, M. (2019). Experience the Red Bull Stratos jump with these AR and VR technologies. Lucerne's Swiss Museum of Transport plays host to a vivid recreation of Felix Baumgartner's record-breaking helium balloon flight and high-altitude skydive from 39km above the Earth. Red Bull Stratos/ Red Bull Content Pool. 26 September. Available at: http://www.redbull.com/int-en/experience-red-bull-stratos-in-new-vr-exhibit

Olenski, S. (2016). Branded content, equity content and why brands need to know the difference. *Forbes.* 24 January. Available at: www.forbes.com/sites/steveolenski/2016/06/24/branded-content-equity-content-and-why-brands-need-to-know-the-difference/#18d428f038ed

Pariser, E. (2011). *The filter bubble: what the internet is hiding from you.* New York: Penguin Books.

Park, H-J., and Yu, S-C. (2019). 이미지 기반 소셜 미디어에서 브랜디드 콘텐츠의 전략적 모호성 광고 효과에 관한 연구, 광고연구. *Advertising Research.* Spring, 120, 5–47.

PQ Media (2018). *Global Branded Entertainment Marketing Forecast 2018.* April. PQ Media LLC.

Price, N. (2012). Branded entertainment: measure the matrix value. *Admap,* February.

Russell, C. A. (2002). Investigating the effectiveness of product placement in television shows: the role of modality and plot connection congruence on brand memory and attitude. *Journal of Consumer Research.* **29,** 306–318.

Russell, C. A. (2007). Advertainment: fusing advertising and entertainment. *Yaffe Center for Persuasive Communication, University of Michigan.* Available at: www.researchgate.net/publication/254351697_Advertainment_Fusing_Advertising_and_Entertainment

Russell, C. A., and Stern, B. B. (2006). Consumers, characters, and products. *Journal of Advertising.* **35**(1), 7–21.

Sheehan, K. B., and Guo, A. (2005). Leaving on a (branded) jet plane: an exploration of audience attitudes towards product assimilation in television content. *Journal of Current Issues & Research in Advertising.* **27**(1), 79–91.

Stewart, R. (2016). Red Bull and GoPro ink exclusive global partnership to inspire the world to live a bigger life. The Drum, 24 May. Available at: www.thedrum.com/news/2016/05/24/red-bull-and-gopro-ink-exclusive-globalpartnership-inspire-world-live-bigger-life

Turner, K. J. (2004). Insinuating the product into the message: an historical context for product placement. *Journal of Promotion Management.* **10**(1/2), 9–14.

Turow, J. (2011). *The daily you: how the new advertising industry is defining your identity and your worth.* New Haven and London: Yale University Press.

Van Loggerenberg, M. J-C., Enslin, C., and Terblanche-Smit, M. (2019). Towards a definition for branded entertainment: an exploratory study. *Journal of Marketing Communications.* Published online: 22 July.

Wenner, L. A. (2004). On the ethics of product placement in media entertainment. In: M-L. Galician, ed. *Handbook of product placement in the mass media*. New York: Hayworth Press, pp. 101–132.

Wharton, C. (2015). *Advertising: critical approaches*. Abingdon, Oxon and New York: Routledge.

World Advertising Research Centre (WARC) (2020). Global entertainment industry saw record revenues in 2019. News. 13 March. Available at: www.warc.com/newsandopinion/news/globalentertainmentindustrysaw recordrevenuesin2019/43361?utm_source=daily-email-free-link&utm_medium=email&utm_campaign=daily-email-emea-prospects-20200313

Yu, H., and Kim, W. (2018). A study of online advertising regulation: focused on experts' perception of advertising with non-commercial content. 광고학 연구 *The Korean Journal of Advertising*. **29**(1), 79–105.

3 Branded entertainment in practice

This chapter will seek to explore the origins, development, and recent examples of branded entertainment in Korea. First, it will briefly review the early stage of branded entertainment in Korea since the mid-2000s. It will then discuss selected campaigns from 2013 to 2019, based on my primary research. Over 30 cases were collected during 2018–2019, covering seven different formats: music/music videos, web drama, web movie, brand webtoon, web reality/entertainment show, advergame, and creator contents. These cases will illustrate the ways in which media and marketing integration evolved in the Korean context. As discussed earlier in the book, both affirmative and critical perspectives coexist in the extant research related to branded entertainment. This chapter will unfold the wider context and varied texts of real-life examples, informed by both perspectives. In the Western critical scholarship, some hold the view of branded entertainment as 'progressive encroaching advertising messages into media content and obscured persuasion' that has become 'pervasive, embedded, and subtle' (Einstein, 2016: 4, 28, 31). Little has been said about whether or not, and to what extent, this is the case in emerging, non-Western markets such as Korea.

One of the earliest branded entertainment-driven campaigns in Korea is the *Anymotion* project for the Samsung mobile phone range Anycall in 2005. A singer named Lee Hyo-Ri released a song titled 'Anymotion' which became number one on the music charts in March and April 2005 (Kim, 2009). Although the song was critiqued for 'blatant commercialism' (Fowler, 2005), it played a significant role in achieving over a 70 per cent increase in consumer preference towards Anycall among Koreans (Kim, 2009: 17). 'Anymotion' music videos were downloadable free of charge on Anycall's official websites, cable channels, and mobiles. Mobile contents such as online 3D dance videos and 'Anymotion'-themed ringtones further encouraged consumer participation in on- and off-line events (e.g. cover dance contest) (Kim,

2009). Three more campaigns followed the *Anymotion* project: a 12-minute-long 'music drama' (a hybrid between music video and drama) titled *Anyclub* (2005); a sequel, *Anystar* (2006); and a project band called Anyband (2007) (Seo, 2015). All of these included K-pop stars well known in Asia at the time such as 2NE1, BoA, TVXQ's Shia Junsu, and Tablo (*Hankyung Daily*, 2007). This served as a foundation for more branded entertainment contents for Samsung mobile phones: for example, a reality show called *Haptic Mission* (2009) and a music video titled *AMOLED Song* (2009) (Lee, 2010).

The automobile and telecommunication were the two most prominent sectors in terms of early adoption of branded entertainment clearly distinguished from traditional product placement. This is evidenced by a series of campaigns in the *Anymotion* project as well as ad movies by the carmakers Kia and SsangYong Motor. Kia's Lotze *Identity* (2006) is referred to as the first ad movie in Korea (Kim, 2010). Following this, SsangYong Motor introduced a short film called *U-turn* (2008), consisting of four parts which were five minutes each (SsangYong Motor, 2008). Both films starred celebrities: the late Kim Ju-Hyuk in *Identity* and So Ji-Seop and Lee Yeon-hui in *U-turn*. They also gained much attention from consumers and marketers as the then 'new' advertising and marketing technique (Jun, 2016; SsangYong Motor, 2008). In a comparative study, Jun (2016) found that *Identity* used rational appeals and messages about the car's features, while *U-turn* focused on storytelling about the relationship between the characters in the movie (Jun, 2016). The first recognition of Korean branded entertainment at the Cannes Festival was that of pizza brand Mister Pizza's *The true origins of pizza* (2012) campaign. This campaign won bronze in the 'Branded Content & Entertainment' category for humorous storytelling about how pizza came from Korean traditional cuisine (Jun, 2016).

Thus, the emergence of branded entertainment was noticeable in the media and marketing industries in Korea since the mid-2000s, but it was embraced by the market leaders in only a handful of product sectors. One of the advantages of product placement and branded entertainment was said to be the relatively low cost in comparison to mainstream above-the-line advertising (Lehu, 2009). However, the cost factor did not seem to appeal to small or medium-sized brands in Korea. More recent examples in the next section will demonstrate branded entertainment became more widely used, mature, and sophisticated to a certain extent.

Music/music video

Product or brand integration in K-pop is not uncommon. As the production costs for music videos increased, entertainment companies pursued financial support from brands. Traditional product placements often took place in K-pop music videos: for example, boy band EXO's music video *Call Me Baby* featured Samsung's headphone range, Level On Wireless, extensively (Samsung Newsroom, 2015). Another form of brand integration was to have K-pop stars perform either a newly produced or a reproduced song in traditional TV spot advertising. An example for this is Korean food manufacturing company Ottogi's ramen snack Bbushuh Bbushu, for which the boy band SHINee modelled in 2009 and 2016 (Ottogi, 2016). Lastly, there is the case of branded entertainment whereby a whole new music piece and a video are produced to promote a product or brand. This section considers the last category, using four examples: Maeil Bio x MAMAMOO, Lotte Chilsung X WJMK, Pepsi x YDPP, and Korean Air X SuperM.

The girl band MAMAMOO's song titled 'Everyday' was launched in March 2018 for the dairy brand Maeil Bio. An advertising agency, RBW, and a production company, RBW M&C, collaborated on this campaign, which consisted of an 'Everyday' music video and a #Bio x #MAMAMOO wedding singer event (e.g. viewers' stories selected for a competition to win a performance by MAMAMOO of 'Everyday' at their wedding) (RBW M&C, 2018). Participation and personalisation are the tools marketers use to sustain a long-term relationship, particularly with ever-important millennials (Einstein, 2016: 48). The *Everyday* YouTube video recorded 1.69 million views and 67k likes as of 10 January 2020. Maeil Bio had already been using promotional videos to reach out to a wide-ranging target audience in terms of age (Maeil Bio, 2020). However, this campaign was different because it specifically targeted younger consumers in their 20s and 30s with branded entertainment suitable for mobile consumption. The wedding event was also apt for this age group. In comparison to Maeil Bio's previous campaigns using traditional TV spot advertising and print advertisements, this collaboration with a K-pop girl band showed higher reach and brand recall amongst younger target audiences (Yoon, 2019).

Maeil Bio's case set the trend for competitors in the beverage sector such as Lotte Chilsung and Pepsi. A project band named WJMK (Wuju Meki) was made up of two members from the girl group Cosmic Girls (or WJSN) and two members from Weki Meki to launch a song titled 'Strong' to promote Lotte Chilsung's drink range Strong (Lee, E-J., 2018). Another four-member project band, YDPP (from two different entertainment companies), was formed while modelling for Pepsi's promotions in Asia: for example, YDPP's song 'Love it Live it' and the music video were released in 2018, followed by fan meetings in Thailand and Taiwan (Lee, E-J., 2018). Pepsi also hosted a concert called 'LOVE IT. LIVE IT. PEPSI CONCERT; starring YDPP and a dozen more

K-pop musicians in November 2018 (Dong, 2018). In the cases of Lotte Chilsung and Pepsi, multiple players operate at multiple levels: entertainment companies, the musicians themselves, the producers of music and music videos, advertising and production agencies, and the brands themselves. Here, we witness the complex nature of merging entertainment, media, and promotion in relation to the accountability of branded entertainment, ownership of intellectual property, and control of the content creation process.

Another example is a recent collaboration between Korean Air and one of the biggest entertainment companies in Korea, SM Entertainment. The outcome was Korean Air's safety video, featuring K-pop artists such as BoA and a boy band called SuperM. Launched in November 2019, this video was attention grabbing (Chen, 2019), but it also sparked controversy because some found it distracting to have too much music (in fact, it was a mix of five music genres such as hip-hop, R&B, electronic, deep house, and synth pop) in a safety video (Cho, K.-H., 2019). However, a Korean Air spokesperson said, 'safety does not have to be serious or boring', reflecting on entertainment or sports-themed safety videos by other airlines (e.g. United Airlines' Star Wars-themed video or Air New Zealand's Lord of the Rings-themed video and rugby-themed video) (Chen, 2019; Korean Air, 2019). The safety video's song 'Let's Go Everywhere' was released as a single album, the profits of which are directed to the Global Poverty Project's Global Citizen campaign to this day (Korean Air, 2019). As of 10 January 2020, this safety video had recorded 13.9 million views and 264k likes (Korean Air X SuperM Safety Video, 2019).

It is interesting to consider the ways in which entertainment companies and brands became co-dependent in various aspects of their businesses. Advertisers and marketers provide financial support for entertainment companies which, in turn, facilitate content creation via K-pop idols; as a result, they both promote their brands. In all the above cases, there were explicit links between the music/music video and the brands (e.g. product name used as the song title). Maeil Bio and Korean Air featured existing bands, whereas Lotte Chilsung and Pepsi had project bands specially formed for the campaigns. This is a clear example of what Kang (2015) termed 'hypercommodification' and 'hyperrationalisation' resulting in the de-individualisation of K-pop idols. The question remains to what extent the audience and musicians themselves perceive this highly rationalised business practice as authentic as non-branded music.

Over the years, the association between music/music video and the brand it promotes has become less distinctively recognisable but, as shown in the above examples, the link between the two still seems explicit. There seem to be more prominent formats for branded entertainment in Korea such as web dramas and brand webtoons (as we will discuss later in this chapter), but music has a greater potential thanks to the growing recognition and popularity of K-pop around the world. It is for this reason that not only domestic brands but also international sportswear brands like Adidas, Puma, Nike, and Reebok, and luxury brands including Gucci, YSL, and Fendi have partnered with K-pop bands (Sinha, 2018). In addition, the scope of K-pop's involvement in promotional activities has widened. The Korean wave has been used extensively in nation branding (Huang, 2011) and also in city branding: for example, BTS was appointed Honorary Ambassadors of Seoul in 2017 (Kim, 2018). It is, however, crucial to reflect on the critique of the increasing level of commercialism and the myths of K-pop. In recent years, there has been a spate of suicides and high-profile sex scandals involving K-pop stars, which raised questions about sexism, cyberbullying, trolling, and unfair, long-term contracts (BBC News, 2019). Critics have said that, together with high societal expectations about K-pop idols' behaviour and appearance, the country's gender and social norms put too much pressure on K-pop idols and trainees (Tai, 2020). It is therefore critical for marketers to acknowledge recent developments in the K-pop industry which could potentially affect consumer reception.

Web drama

A recent development of digital content in Korea is the web drama format (Kang, 2017: 762, 768). Web dramas are original serialised dramas that usually run for five to ten minutes per episode. They are released primarily on online platforms and are easy to watch on mobile devices. The popularity of web dramas has been growing thanks to non-linear viewing patterns with younger Koreans as the main target audience (Kim, M-J., 2019; Park, J-C., 2018). The web drama seems to be one of the most frequently used formats for branded entertainment. The next section illustrates how widely this branded entertainment strategy has been used across different product sectors: food, supermarket, retail, and electronics.

A web drama series titled *7 First Kisses* by Lotte Duty Free (of the retail corporation Lotte Group) aimed to address a challenge arising from Korea's geopolitical and diplomatic situations with China (Lotte Duty Free, 2016). China's ban on all group travel to Korea as part of its response to Korea's decision to deploy the US Terminal High

Altitude Area Defense (THAAD) missile system in early 2017 had a major impact on tourism and Lotte Duty Free's sales (Premack 2017)[1]. China objected to the THAAD system on the grounds that its radar could penetrate Chinese territory and undermine regional security (Reuters, 2017).

Duty free has been an important component in the industry as Korea overtook Britain in 2010 to become the world's biggest duty-free market, and the above diplomatic spat has hit the industry hard (Reuters, 2017). At least 79 of Lotte's 99 supermarkets in China have been closed as a result of the row (Premack, 2017). Furthermore, the domestic duty-free market has been oversaturated and rising competition has meant store closures for some (e.g. Hyundai Paint Co Ltd's Duty Free and Hanwha Galleria Timeworld Co Ltd) and pay cuts for others (e.g. Lotte Duty Free) (Reuters, 2017). The objectives of the *7 First Kisses* campaign were twofold: first, to re-establish brand image as the market leader for domestic consumers and Lotte employees; and second, to actively promote Lotte Duty Free to Chinese tourists in a less intrusive advertising format featuring Korean wave stars (Park, J-C., 2018). All eight episodes were released on Naver TV (provided by the biggest portal in Korea; Naver), YouTube, and Facebook as well as Yuku and Weibo, which are Chinese SNS platforms. It recorded over 120 million views on Weibo only, which led to the Chinese production of a *7 First Kisses* parody (Park, J-C., 2018).

In the food and supermarket sector, E Mart's web drama series *My Precious World* (E Mart, 2017) is one of the well-known examples because of its storytelling and immediate effect on sales. E Mart is the oldest and largest retailer and discount store in Korea, owned by Samsung's retail arm, Shinsegae Department Store (E Mart, 2020). The first episode of *My Precious World* was about a not-so-rich young couple and E Mart's over 400 kinds of 'world beer (imported beer)', where a wife said, 'Just buy one of each' (one of each for her and the husband) and the husband bought one of each type, all 400 kinds. Following the episode's release in August 2017, within a month, the sales of the 'world beer' category increased by 29.5 per cent (Son, 2017). Two agencies collaborated on this campaign; Interstella was responsible for the idea creation and the media placement, and Dolphiners oversaw the production (Park, L-M., 2018). 'Empathy' was the key part in the planning to provide a brand experience which the audiences could empathise with and react to (e.g. like, reply, and share) (Spikes Asia, 2018). As of 10 January 2020, the overall accumulated views on various platforms went over 5 million, with 1.1 million views on Facebook and 700k views on YouTube.

Another case study is with the ramen market leader Nongshim's *Some Boiling Time*. In April 2018, it started on only one platform, the company's own YouTube channel, but within a month it was expanded to Nongshim's other SNS channels, IPTV, and TV commercials (Group IDD 2018). As of 10 January 2020, a YouTube video clip with all eight episodes of *Some Boiling Time* recorded 1.68 million views and 13k likes (Ramen Gongjakso, 2018). This led to a sequel web drama, *Somestery Share House* (Ramen Gongjakso, 2019), and viewers voted online to determine the storyline of the following episode (Kim, S-H., 2019). Since its inception, Nongshim's in-house PR continued to produce not only web dramas but also more hybrid contents such as web sitcoms and web talk shows. The sense of continuity in engaging with consumers contributed to Nongshim's effective running of the YouTube channel's 'Ramen Gongjakso', which has 53k subscribers (Ramen Gongjakso, 2020). It is worth recognising that the brand itself rather than a specialist agency produced, consistently, good quality branded entertainment using a centralised and integrated web contents channel like 'Ramen Gongjakso'.

Nongshim's case is relatively rare in that the brand funds, produces, and distributes branded content across its paid and owned media, controlling a sense of having full ownership. A closer look at the comments on 'Ramen Gongjakso' reveals a strong sense of consumer engagement: for example, there is active involvement by the viewers, especially millennials and post-millennials, to determine the narrative flow and plot. Nongshim recently had an unexpected sales boost via the 2020 Oscar winner *Parasite*. There was no product placement deal between Nongshim and the film production (Ahn, 2020), but a mix of two Nongshim instant noodles, 'Chapaguri (or Jjapaguri)', (translated as 'Ram-don', meaning the combination of ramen and udon) was used as an important motif in the movie. After the news of the award broke, its share price rose by 4.46 per cent in two days, and there were more than 100 YouTube videos by international movie fans of the 'Chapaguri' recipe (Chung, 2020).

To sum up, branded entertainment in the format of the web drama seems to provide a sense of continuity for readers, facilitating a more interactive relationship and participation. This is an inherent advantage of this newly emerged medium as an effective promotional tool because it is conveniently packaged for contemporary viewers in 'snack culture', in Jin's (2020) terms.

Web movie

A web movie (or ad movie) is a format where we can find some pioneering works of branded entertainment in both global and local contexts: for example, BMW's *The Hire* series (2001–2002), Kia's

Identity (2006), and SsangYong Motor's *U-turn* (2008). This section examines two recent examples which are not car brands.

Premiered in December 2017, Samsung Electronics' web movie *Two Lights: Relúmĭno* could look like an unbranded film because there is no direct mention or description of the brand or product. The *Relúmĭno* app is a visual aid application developed by Samsung's in-house incubator programme C-Lab (Creative Lab) that is freely downable from its home page (Samsung Newsroom, 2017). Although there are product placements of Samsung's Gear VR headsets, smartphones, and monitors in the movie, one could say this is done in a subtle and not-so-intrusive manner. Inspired by the fact that about 86 per cent of visually impaired people worldwide have low vision, this movie talks about how two young people at a photography club for the visually impaired learn to take their own photos, growing closer to each other while doing so (Two Lights: Relúmĭno, 2017). By March 2020, it had over 24 million views and 23k likes on YouTube. To put this into context, the smartphone business worldwide has been stagnating, and among the three biggest makers (Samsung, Apple, and Huawei), only Huawei's sales are growing (Stout 2019). As the worldwide declining smartphone sales hit Samsung, it needed to go beyond the technology and innovation heritage and rearticulate its core values around a brand purpose (Campaign Brief Asia, 2018). Hence, *Two Lights: Relúmĭno* attempted to help maintain Samsung's positioning as an innovator while rebuilding the brand based on a purpose, not just in terms of functionalities but also empowerment (Singh, 2017). The movie won gold in the Innovation category at Spikes Asia in 2018 (Campaign Brief Asia, 2018).

More recently, in July 2019, OB (Oriental Brewery) launched an interactive film titled *AORB*. The interactive film is a new genre.[2] This format was highly appropriate for the core message in this campaign, choice. Founded in 1933, OB Beer is one of the oldest and largest brands in the beverage sector in Korea. It is now a subsidiary of a multinational drink and brewing company based in Belgium, AB InBev (Anheuser-Busch InBev SA/NV). *AORB* was an integral part of OB's IMC campaign titled *YAASS*. The title of this interactive film came from 'Choose A or B', sending out the brand message of 'We support your choice' (Lee, 2019). The domestic beer market had been going through an oversupply and a sales decline since the mid-2010s (Jung, 2018). Since 2006, OB Beer has also introduced such a wide range of products (e.g. six variations – Cass Fresh, Cass Ice Light, Cass 2X, Cass Red, Cass Beats, and Cass Lemon – in the OB Cass range only), so 'choice' was an important theme. *AORB* was Korea's first interactive film production in collaboration with YouTube, using YouTube's end screen feature (Lee,

2019). Viewers were invited to choose actions five times during a seven-minute-long movie, and each choice led to a different ending. *AORB* surpassed 5 million YouTube views within a month of the launch (Kim, J-H., 2019).

The above cases seem impactful in their own ways, whether it is about promoting an intangible product such as a visual aid application or experimenting with a novel genre like an interactive film. However, despite the early presence of the ad movie (or web movie) format in branded entertainment, not many brands have opted for this approach.

Brand webtoon

Webtoons – a portmanteau of web and cartoons – have been a staple of popular culture in Korea for over a decade (Bae, 2017: 73). Due to the convergence of digital technologies and popular culture such as *manhwa* (cartoons in Korean), webtoons have been one of the major cultural forms representing everyday life and culture (Jin, 2015). While Korea is not the only country to enjoy webtoons, it is the first country to create a new form of *manwha* by utilising major characteristics of digital technologies (Jin, 2015: 193). Unlike *manwha* or Japanese manga, webtoons are optimised for smartphones and PCs, with vertical scrolling and in full colour (Osaki, 2019). In the early 2000s, the socio-economic milieu surrounding the Korean *manhwa* industry substantially changed, resulting in the beginning of the boom of webtoons (Jin, 2020). Daum and Naver created webtoon portals in the early 2000s. A Korean National Assembly audit released in December 2019 shows that the number of Naver visitors was 31.25 million for Naver and 27.11 million for Daum, compared to 19.73 million for Google and 10.47 million for YouTube (Kim, J-Y. 2020).

The Hanwha Chemical brand webtoon *God of Annual Salary* (*Yeon Bong Shin* in Korean) provides an interesting case study. Hanwha Chemical is a B2B company in the petrochemical sector, which does not often use branded entertainment to target consumers. In addition, for corporate PR webtoons, *God of Annual Salary* was considerably longer than any other series. It ran almost for a year (from 16 July 2013 to 10 June 2014) with 22 episodes (Hanwha Solution, 2013). Featuring a protagonist, Bong Shin, who was hired by Hanwha Chemical accidentally through a clerical error, the series aimed to portray Hanwha Chemical as a familiar and personable brand and the petrochemical industry as not a boring but a dynamic business.

A recent study of 50 Korean webtoons from 2012 to 2017 revealed that there was a disconnect between the type of message strategy used in brand webtoons and consumer preference (Lee and Hwang, 2017). For example, the most frequently used message strategy was based on the information, but consumers responded most favourably to an emotional transition. In the case of *God of Annual Salary*, both elements – information and emotion – were used effectively to engage with consumers over a long period.

Webtoons have also been used by public service campaigns. The Ministry of Health and Welfare sponsored a ten-episode-long webtoon series about anti-smoking, primarily for teenagers, in 2015. It is worth recognising that earlier in the same year, the government's 44-second anti-smoking advertisement angered smokers' groups, which led to a public protest (BBC News 2015). By contrast, this webtoon series was well received and tolerated, with nearly 5 million accumulative views and the average number of comments reaching 1 million per episode (Kim, 2016). The Ministry of Economy and Finance also ran an eight-episode-long webtoon series about budgeting in 2019. Both webtoons were distributed by Naver Webtoon.

More recently, Big Hit Entertainment and Naver Webtoon collaborated on the BTS webtoon series titled *The Most Beautiful Moment in Life Pt. 0: Save Me* about the friendship and fate of seven boys, who take on the real names of BTS members. It ran from January to April 2019, in seven countries around the world, recording over 50 million accumulative views (Park, J-H., 2019). This is a case of K-pop idols promoting themselves as a brand rather than being used as a vehicle to represent another brand.

Web reality/entertainment show

Highschool Styleicon is a survival audition programme for high school students, which is produced by Blank Corporation and broadcast via YouTube (SM Entertainment, 2019). The winners can collaborate with beauty and fashion brands and launch their own brands (Min, 2019). In Season 1 (from June to July 2019), 13 participants lived in the same house while carrying out different missions such as styling webtoon characters and music video cast. As of February 2020, Season 2 was in production.

Often referred to as 'V (video) Commerce leader' in Korea, Blank Corporation was the first to introduce the concept of 'contents commerce' to the country whereby the company develops, manufactures, and promotes a product, using video contents on SNS platforms (Cho, D-J., 2019). What is important in *Highschool Styleicon* is to discover 'micro-influencers' for Blank Corporation and its products. The fact that this show's premise is not just to find young talents but also to develop future micro-influencers for the brand raises some ethical concerns. Not only are most of the participants underage, but the activity of 'branding an individual' raises conceptual, practical, and ethical issues (Khamis et al., 2017: 192). MacDonald (2014: 147) argues that social media fame prompts young people to focus on image and artifice at the expense of 'real' achievements of depth and substance, and that this can be articulated through a false and materialistic grandiosity. Some industry literature considers micro-influencers as 'the voice of the public' (Tait, 2017), creating 'more authentic' content and driving higher levels of engagement with consumers (Tesseras, 2018). However, this can be problematic for consumers because influencers do not always disclose sponsored contents. Although more and more influencers use #ad and #spon, it is difficult to identify sponsored contents without the publishers' own disclosure. Although the *Public Notice of Imposing Fine on Violations of the Fair Labelling and Advertising Act 2012* has been revised, this is an area where regulation is difficult. This is discussed in greater detail in the next chapter.

Advergame

One of the important forms of branded entertainment is advergaming (Lehu, 2009; Wise et al., 2008; Janes, 2020). Dahl, Eagle, and Baez (2009) described advergames as electronic games with embedded commercial messages that aim to form an emotional connection between the game and brand featured within it. According to Cauberghe and De Pelsmacker (2000: 5), the advergame format can be distinguished from 'in-game' advertising in the sense that the latter more closely resembles traditional product placement. In contrast, advergames as branded entertainment are specially made to promote the brand, with less complex rules and shorter playing times than a 'real' game, and therefore they can be easily distributed on different platforms such as websites, via email, mobile, and interactive digital TV. In a way, advergames are a rare context in which the players are aware that these games are promotional content when they opt in. Hence, they are often more willing to tolerate the advertising content than they would be with an uninvited pop-up advertisement (Dahl, Eagle, and Baez, 2009). It is claimed that the advergame format is more likely to secure heightened attention, high engagement, the ability to reach a young demographic, and length of exposure (Taylor, 2019).

SK Telecom's *5GX Boost Park* campaign was launched in July 2019. It aimed to raise the awareness about '5G Cluster' where new technologies such as augmented reality (AR), virtual reality (VR), and artificial intelligence (AI) converge, using SK's Ultra Dense Networks (Jung, 2019). In addition to eight kinds of 5G B2B clusters (e.g. 5G Factory, 5G Smart Hospital, 5G Smart Logistics and Distribution, Smart City, Media, Public Safety, Smart Office, and Defense), SK opened the 5G Boost Park in ten commercial districts across the country. In the *5GX Boost Park*, visitors can have AR//VR- and AI-assisted gaming experiences in different zones such as the 5G Roll Park, AR Zoo, and 5G Stadium. 'Flow' is an important factor in brand experience involving advergaming (Hernandez, 2011), and the 5GX Boost Parks provide an atypical example, offering a sense of flow to visitors across on- and off-line using AR- and VR-assisted experiences.

In Korea, advergames are also often referred to as 'branded mini-games' (Park, H-S., 2019). There were several branded mini-games in the mid-2010s: for example, a 2015 social commerce advergame called *Society* by a Korean ginseng company, WonKi Sansam; the Kookmin Bank's *The Challenge* in 2017; and Kia's *The Master Racing Challenge* to promote a new SUV (sport unitality vehicle) in 2019. However, this format has not become mainstream within the branded entertainment industry. It seems that in a country known worldwide for its culture of massively multiplayer online role-playing games (MMORPG) (Jin, 2017), 'mini' games do not attract a large audience.

Creator contents

An alcoholic beverage brand, HiteJinro's *Chamisul Live* (from December 2015 to December 2018), was a series of live footages of musicians at social scenes, with impromptu music and soju *Chamisul* (a traditional Korean liquor). The content agency NEWEARLY collaborated with Dingo Music for this hybridised form of native advertising, product placement, and branded entertainment. *Chamisul Live* is a new format even within the branded entertainment category as it is not exactly a piece of music/music video nor is it an ongoing reality/entertainment show. Usually the setting is a private drinking scene among well-known musicians where they end up sharing some music. Here, the sense of privacy and immediacy appealed to viewers, and in 2016 it won the gold at the International Business Awards as Marketing Campaign of the Year and the silver in the Branded Content Campaign of the Year (International Business Awards, 2016). On the other hand, this raises ethical concerns around underage binge drinking and alcohol misuse. Livestreaming and YouTube videos attract many viewers of a young age, and this type of branded entertainment could instil a highly glamorised and romanticised idea of a drinking culture into young people's minds, influencing their long-term attitudes towards alcohol.

Over the years, the regulatory measures against alcohol advertising in Korea has been strengthened. The Ministry of Health and Welfare and the Korea Health Promotion Institute announced the *Drinking Damage Prevention Action Plan* in 2018, which led to the revision of the *National Health Promotion Act* by the Ministry of Health and Welfare in 2019 (Korea Health Promotion Institute, 2019). Under this revised act, from 2020, there will be a ban on alcohol advertising in public transport, and more media channels will be subject to 'no alcohol advertising between 7 a.m. and 10 p.m.' (Kim, E-Y., 2019). Currently, this only applies to traditional media such as TV, radio, and cinema, but it will also apply to new media (cable, satellite, and IPTV) under the new legislation.

It is true that branded entertainment provides alternative ways to engage with consumers; however, this strategy should not be treated as a resort to elude regulation. For ethical practice, all parties need to play their parts: for example, improving media literacy and consumer awareness, engaging in self-regulation, and upholding editorial integrity.

Conclusion

Branded entertainment illustrates the way that marketers have sought to co-link entertainment content with new technological infrastructures to give brands greater *credibility, interactivity*, and *depth of appeal* (Grainge, 2011) (emphasis added). While these elements are not exclusive to one another, we can find an emphasis on certain elements in the above campaigns. For example, in Hanwha Chemical's *God of Annual Salary (Yeon Bong Shin)* and Samsung's *Two Lights: Relúmĭno*, it was more important to give greater credibility to the advertised brands because these campaigns promote the intangible, corporate identity of a petrochemical company, Hanwha, and an visual aid application, respectively. Other campaigns focused on interactivity: for example, Nongshim's *Somstery Share House*, SK Telecom's *5GX Boost Park*, and Blank Corporation's *Highschool Styleicon*. Various brands in the retail sector, including alcohol, seemed to emphasise the depth of appeal: for example, Lotte Duty Free's *7 First Kisses*, E Mart's *My Precious World*, and HiteJinro's *Chamisul Live*.

It is also clear that the participatory culture is a prerequisite for effective branded entertainment. Jenkins (2006: 4) states that the term *participatory culture* contrasts with older notions of passive media spectatorship. In the case of the interactive film and web dramas discussed above, we can witness the changing relations between brands and consumers. These consumers act upon the invitation to participate in a production. Nongshim's *Somestery Share House* and OB Beer's *AROB* are good examples. Other events that accompanied branded entertainment (e.g. Maeil Bio x MAMAMOO's wedding singer event or Pepsi's concert) were also made possible due to consumers' active involvement.

Lastly, it is worth recognising how closely brands have been working with the Korean pop culture industry in both domestic and global contexts, whether it is for rebranding and repositioning, or raising awareness. Hyundai's collaboration with BTS, Maeil Bio x MAMAMOO, Korean Air x SuperM, Naver Webtoon x BTS, HiteJinro's *Chamisul Live*, and Lotte Duty Free's *7 First Kisses* are a case in point. Problems of authenticity and creative autonomy have been raised in the case of K-pop project bands which were formed solely on commercial grounds. In addition, some of these brands were intended to advertise alcoholic beverages (e.g. HiteJinro and OB Beer), which is strictly regulated in traditional broadcast and public transport advertising. In contrast to old media, it is more difficult to implement the necessary regulatory measures for new media. Hence, there is a growing concern that more vulnerable groups such as those who are underage or those with less media literacy might become desensitised to alcohol use. The next chapter will examine these ethical questions and regulatory issues.

Notes

1　In this sentence, as has been the case throughout the book, Korea means the Republic of Korea or South Korea.
2　*Black Mirror* was the first interactive film, launched by Netflix in December 2018 (Strause, 2018). The English band Major Lazer's 'Know No Better' (https://eko.com/v/major-lazer), Bob Dylan's CD box set 'Like a Rolling Stone' (https://eko.com/v/like-a-rolling-stone?autoplay=true), and Coldplay's Ink (https://eko.com/v/coldplay-ink?autoplay=true) are some examples of interactive videos used for music promotion.

Bibliography

Ahn, S-H. (2020). '전 세계 스크린에 뜬 '짜파구리...농심 '고마워 기생충', *Chosun Biz*. 11 February. Available at: https://biz.chosun.com/site/data/html_dir/2020/02/11/2020021101808.html?utm_source=naver&utm_medium=original&utm_campaign=biz
Bae, K. Y. B. (2017). From underground to the palm of your hand: The spatiality and cultural practice of South Korean webtoons' *East Asian Journal of Popular Culture*. 3(1), 73–84.

BBC (2015). S Korea: Health ministry advert angers smokers' group. 25 November. Available at: www.bbc.co.uk/news/blogs-news-from-elsewhere-34920754

BBC (2019). Sulli: the woman who rebelled against the K-pop world. 18 October. Available at: www.bbc.co.uk/news/world-asia-50051575

Campaign Brief Asia (2018). BMW Dentsu Sydney wins Grand Prix in the Spikes Asia Innovation Category: Cheil Worldwide South Korea wins Innovation Spike. 28 September. Available at: https://campaignbriefasia. com/2018/09/28/bwm-dentsu-sydney-wins-grand-p-1/

Cauberghe, V., and De Pelsmacker, P. (2000). Advergames: the impact of brand prominence and game repetition on brand responses. *Journal of Advertising.* **39**(1), 5–18.

Chen, J. (2019). Korean Air's new safety video features K-pop artists Super M and BoA. *Business Traveller.* 5 November. Available at: www.businesstraveller. com/business-travel/2019/11/05/korean-airs-new-safety-video-features-k-pop-artists-superm-and-boa/

Cho, D-J. (2019). SNS대란템' 남대광 블랭크코퍼레이션 대표. *Joongang Sisa Magazine* 중앙시사메거진. 23 November. Available at: https://jmagazine. joins.com/forbes/view/328318

Cho, K-H. (2019). 비행기 안전 수칙 영상인가? 아이돌 뮤비인가? 논란의 대한항공 영상. *SBS News.* 12 November. Available at: https://news.sbs. co.kr/news/endPage.do?news_id=N1005519709&plink=ORI&cooper=NAVER

Chung, H-Y. (2020). 기생충으로 뜬 짜파구리…농심도 '오스카 효과' 톡톡. *JoongAng Ilbo.* 11 February. Available at: https://news.joins.com/article/23703430

Dahl, S., Eagle, L., and Baez, C. (2009). Analyzing advergames: Active diversions or actually deception. An exploratory study of online advergames content. *Young Consumers.* **10**, 46–59.

Dong, S-H. (2018). Star-studded PEPSI concert thrills fans. *The Korea Times.* 18 November. Available at: www.koreatimes.co.kr/www/nation/2018/11/682_258867.html

E Mart (2017). 대박 신박한 이마트 광고 – 웹드라마 '나의 소중한 세계. YouTube video, added by Trello Twain [Online]. Available at: www.youtube. com/watch?v=ifaeZt7rTik

E Mart (2020). 이마트 사업구조, 연혁. Available at: www.emartcompany.com/ ko/company/business.do

Einstein, M. (2016). *Black Ops Advertising: Native Ads, Content Marketing and the Covert World of the Digital Sell.* New York: OR Books.

Fowler, G. A. (2005). In Asia, it's nearly impossible to tell a song from an ad. *Pittsburgh Post-Gazette.* 31 May. Available at: www.post-gazette.com/ business/tech-news/2005/05/31/In-Asia-it-s-nearly-impossible-to-tell-a-song-from-an-ad/stories/200505310165

Grainge, P. (2011). A song and dance: branded entertainment and mobile promotion. International Journal of Cultural Studies. 15(2), 165–180.

GROUP IDD (2018). Case studies: Nongshim web drama campaign. 케이스스터디: 농심 웹드라마 영상 캠페인, April. Available at: http://project.groupidd.com/case-studies/view.php?seq=15

Hankyung Daily (2007). 가요계 막강 군단 '애니밴드'전격 공개. 8 November. Available at: www.hankyung.com/life/article/2007110840157

Hanwha Solution (2013). 그것이 알고 싶다! 연봉신 탄생 뒷얘기. *Hanwha Solution/Chemical News*. 10 September. Available at: www.chemidream.com/579

Hernandez, M. D. (2011). A model of flow experience as determinant of positive attitudes toward online advergames. *Journal of Promotion Management*, **17**(3), 315–326.

Huang, S. (2011). Nation-branding and transnational consumption: Japanmania and the Korean wave in Taiwan. *Media, Culture & Society*. **33**(1): 3–18.

International Business Awards (2016). Marketing awards winners. Available at: https://stevieawards.com/iba/marketing-awards-winners-1

Janes, S. (2020). *Alternate reality games: promotion and participatory culture.* Abingdon and New York: Routledge.

Jenkins, H. (2006). *Convergence culture: where old and new media collide.* New York and London: New York University Press.

Jin, D. Y. (2015). Digital convergence of Korea's webtoons: transmedia storytelling. *Communication Research and Practice*. **1**(3), 193–209.

Jin, D. Y. (ed) (2017). *Mobile gaming in Asia: politics, culture and emerging technologies*. Springer.

Jin, D. Y. (2020). *Transmedia storytelling in East Asia: the age of digital media.* Abingdon and New York: Routledge.

Jun, J. W. (2016). 광고와 엔터테인먼트의 경계를 허물다, *Oricom Brand Journal*. 4 July.

Jung, E-S. (2018). 오비맥주, 영업환경 악화에도 1위 지키며 2–3위와 격차 벌려… '메가 브랜드'통했다. *CNB Journal*. 16 November. Available at: http://weekly.cnbnews.com/news/article.html?no=126048

Jung, S-Y. (2019). SKT to create clusters from Seoul to Jeju. *Kore IT Times*. 18 July. Available at: www.koreaittimes.com/news/articleView.html?idxno=91924

Kang, I. (2015). The political economy of idols: South Korea's neoliberal restructuring and its impact on the entertainment labour force In: J- B. Choi and R. Maliangkay, eds. *K-pop: The International Rise of the Korean Music Industry*. New York: Routledge, pp. 51–64.

Kang, J. M. (2017). Just another platform for television? The emerging web dramas as digital culture in South Korea. *Media, Culture & Society*. **39**(5), 762–772.

Khamis, S., Ang, L., and Welling, R. (2017). Self-branding, 'micro-celebrity' and the rise of social media influencers. *Celebrity Studies*. **8**(2), 191–208.

Kim, D. H. (2010). The melody of the film narrative rhythm: focusing on research into the AD-movie 'Identity' and 'U-turn'. 디지털영상학술지 *Preview*. **7**(2), 69–100.

Kim, E-Y. (2019). 술 마시는 '공유' 광고 이제 못본다...주류업계 잇단 규제에 난감. *Chosun.com*. 10 November. Available at: http://news.chosun.com/site/data/html_dir/2019/11/08/2019110803987.html?utm_source=naver&utm_medium=original&utm_campaign=news

Kim, H-B. (2018). BTS to promote Seoul tourism. *Korea Times*. 21 October. Available at: www.koreatimes.co.kr/www/nation/2018/10/281_257357.html

Kim, J-H. (2009). Branded entertainment and Anymotion. *Brand Forum*. 27 May. Available at: https://blog.naver.com/vonchio/110048312265

Kim, J-H. (2019). [2019년 소비자신뢰대상] 카스 '아오르비', 한달 만에 500만뷰...젊은세대 공감 이끌어. *Asia Today*. 28 August. Available at: www.asiatoday.co.kr/view.php?key=20190827010013485

Kim, J-Y. (2020). Google Korea searches for answers. *JoongAng Daily*. 15 January. Available at: https://koreajoongangdaily.joins.com/news/article/article.aspx?aid=2983581

Kim, M-J. (2019). '내 얘기잖아?' 웹드라마 열풍...1020 사로잡은 비결은? *Sedaily* 서울경제. 14 July. Available at: www.sedaily.com/NewsView/1VLOVDYAEI

Kim, S-H. (2019). 농심 웹드라마 '썸스테리 쉐어하우스', 라면 이야기 재미있게 끓여드리겠습니다. *Digital Insight*. 7 March. Available at: https://ditoday.com/%EB%86%8D%EC%8B%AC-%EC%9B%B9%EB%93%9C%EB%9D%BC%EB%A7%88-%EC%8D%88%EC%8A%A4%ED%85%8C%EB%A6%AC-%EC%89%90%EC%96%B4%ED%95%98%EC%9A%B0%E C%8A%A4-%EB%9D%BC%EB%A9%B4-%EC%9D%B4%EC%95%BC/

Kim, Y-N. (2016). [집중취재] 딱딱한 내용도 쉽게... '재미·홍보' 두 토끼 잡다. *Segye Ilbo*. 18 October. Available at: www.segye.com/newsView/20161018003015

Korea Health Promotion Institute (2019). 음주폐해예방 실행계획. 10 January. Available at: www.khealth.or.kr/board/view?pageNum=1&rowCnt=8&no1=80&linkId=998977&menuId=MENU00664&schType=0&schText=&boardStyle=Gallery&categoryId=&continent=&country=

Korean Air (2019). Korean Air unveils all-new safety video starring K-pop group SuperM'. Press Release. 4 November. Available at: www.koreanair.com/global/en/about/news/press_release/2019_11_safetyvideo/

Korean Air X SuperM Safety Video (2019) YouTube video, added by Korean Air [Online]. Available at: https://www.youtube.com/watch?v=8lSbPWn_6R4

Lee, E-J. (2018) 'YDPP, 우주미키, 브랜드와 손잡은 이색 유닛 바람', *Yonhap News*, 4 June. Available at: https://www.yna.co.kr/view/AKR20180602044100005?input=1195m

Lee, G-L. (2019). Interactive film 'AORB' offers viewers to choose story. *The Korea Times*. 15 July. Available at: www.koreatimes.co.kr/www/art/2020/02/689_272308.html

Lee, K-B. (2010). 슈퍼스타K2 톱4, 갤탭 브랜디드 마케팅. *Yonhap News*. 30 December. Available at: https://news.naver.com/main/read.nhn?mode=LSD&mid=sec&sid1=105&oid=001&aid=0004843469

Lee, J., and Hwang, J-S. (2017). Characteristics of and consumers' responses to brand webtoons. 광고연구 *Advertising Research*. Winter, 115, 246–296.

Lehu, J-M. (2009). *Branded entertainment: Product placement & brand strategy in the entertainment business*. London and Philadelphia: Kogan Page.

Lotte Duty Free (2016). 7 First Kisses 첫 키스만 일곱번째. YouTube video, added by lottedutyfree. Available at: www.youtube.com/watch?v=9vMwB0f zQcg&list=PLMhlGgdYksJ6iUWT4D7liEm6Hv27VJll1

MacDonald, P. (2014). Narcissism in the modern world. *Psychodynamic Practice*. **20**(2), 144–153.

Maeil Bio (2020). Maeil Dairies: PR Promotional Videos. Available at: www. maeil.com/eng/news/video_tv.jsp

Mamamoo_Everyday (2018). YouTube video, added by 1theK [Online]. Available at: www.youtube.com/watch?v=LbWt67vVNgc [Accessed 5 February 2020].

Min, H-B. (2019). [인터뷰] 고간지 제작사 '블랭크' 콘텐츠커머스 선두... 3년새 매출 2900% 폭풍성장. *Kyeonggi Ilbo*. 30 October. Available at: www. kyeonggi.com/news/articleView.html?idxno=2187544

Osaki, T. (2019). South Korea's booming 'webtoons' put Japan's print manga on notice. *The Japan Times*. 5 May. Available at: www.japantimes.co.jp/news/ 2019/05/05/business/tech/south-koreas-booming-webtoons-put-japans-print-manga-notice/#.XqSQsmhKg2w

Ottogi (2016). 2016 오뚜기 뿌셔뿌셔 – 샤이니 TV-CF 30초. YouTube video, added by Ottoginoodle [Online]. Available at: www.youtube.com/ watch?v=j6iSFRUSPy4

Parasite Choi Woo Shik AORB by Cass (2019). YouTube video, added by Cass [Online]. Available at: www.youtube.com/watch?v=TOv-Uq7XffM

Park, J-C. (2018). A study on usefulness of web drama for corporate PR: focusing on the viewer commentary of web drama 'Only the First Kiss Seventh' 기업PR용 웹드라마의 유용성 연구 – 웹드라마 <첫 키스만 일곱 번째>의 시청자 댓글 중심으로. MA thesis, Seoul: Hongik University.

Park, J. H. (2019). BTS becomes cultural phenomenon. *The Korea Times*. 28 January. Available at www.koreatimes.co.kr/www/nation/2019/01/682_ 262792.html

Park, L-M. (2018). 이마트, 브랜드에 숨을 불어넣다. *Korea Herald Business* 해럴드경제. 19 April. Available at: http://heraldk.com/2018/04/19/ %EC%9D%B4%EB%A7%88%ED%8A%B8-%EB%B8%8C%EB%9E%9C %EB%93%9C%EC%97%90-%EC%88%A8%EC%9D%84-%EB%B6%88% EC%96%B4%EB%84%A3%EB%8B%A4/

Premack, R. (2017). A row with China over U.S. missiles is devastating South Korea's tourism industry. *Time*. 11 April. Available at: https://time.com/ 4734066/south-korea-tourism-china-thaad/

Ramen Gongjakso (2018). 썸 끓는 시간, YouTube video, added by Ramen Gongjakso [Online]. Available at: www.youtube.com/watch?v=YwpdzP05zcc

Ramen Gongjakso (2019). 썸하우스, YouTube video, added by Ramen Gongjakso [Online]. Available at: www.youtube.com/watch?v=6rvnsr2jVq M&feature=youtu.be

Ramen Gongjakso (2020). YouTube channel, added by Ramen Gongjakso [Online]. Available at: www.youtube.com/channel/UC2jcRm9-QL43ibuc bQIZoc5w

RBW M&C (2018). [매일유엽] 마마무의 매일봐요 웨딩싱어 이벤트 사연읽기편'. Available at: www.rbwmnc.com/?act=board&bbs_code= portfolio&category_code=0401&bbs_mode=view&bbs_seq=82

Reuters (2017). S.Korea's Hanwha to close duty free store as Chinese tourists stay away. 3 July. Available at: www.reuters.com/article/hgtc-china/s-koreas-hanwha-to-close-duty-free-store-as-chinese-tourists-stay-away-idUSL3N1JU2PW

Samsung Newsroom (2015). 엑소가 선택한 잇 아이템_③ 시우민의 음악 파트너, 레벨 온 와이어리스. 8 April. Available at: https://news.samsung.com/kr/%EC%97%91%EC%86%8C%EA%B0%80-%EC%84%A0%ED%83%9D%ED%95%9C-%EC%9E%87-%EC%95%84%EC%9D%B4%ED%85%9C_%E2%91%A2-%EC%8B%9C%EC%9A%B0%EB%AF%BC%EC%9D%98-%EC%9D%8C%EC%95%85-%ED%8C%8C%ED%8A%B8%EB%84%88-%EB%A0%88

Samsung Newsroom (2017). [Video] Samsung premieres short film, 'Two Lights: Relúmĭno'. 21 December. Available at: https://news.samsung.com/global/video-samsung-premieres-short-film-two-lights-relumino

Seo, K-W. (2015). *소셜 미디어와 SNS 마케팅*. Seoul: Communication Books.

Singh, S. (2017). Samsung innovation chief: define your brand purpose, not just brand promise. *Campaign*. 3 July. Available at: www.campaignlive.co.uk/article/samsung-innovation-chief-define-brand-purpose-not-just-brand-promise/1438337

Sinha, K. (2018). Asian youth in 2019: K-Pop, wellness, sustainability and Bollywood goes to China. *Admap*. December.

SM Entertainment (2019). Super star stylist Han Hye Yeon, Blank TV *Highschool Styleicon*'. Press Centre. 17 June. Available at: www.smentertainment.com/PressCenter/Details/3161

Son, I-S. (2017). 20–30에 더 가까이... 웹드라마 만드는 이마트. *Maekyung* 매일경제. 11 October. Available at: www.mk.co.kr/news/business/view/2017/10/671506/

Spikes Asia (2018). Winners: digital – my precious world. Available at: www2.spikes.asia/winners/2018/interactive/entry.cfm?entryid=1165&award=101&order=1&direction=1

SsangYong Motor (2008). The Actyon and Actyon Sports come together with a film for new advertisements. *SsangYong Motor News*. 14 April. Available at: www.smotor.com/en/med_cen/news/1205587_13941.html

Stout, K. L. (2019). A rare look inside Samsung's secretive ideas lab. *CNN Business*. 17 September. Available at: https://edition.cnn.com/interactive/2019/09/business/samsung-headquarters-south-korea/index.html

Strause, J. (2018). 'Black Mirror' interactive film: inside the 2-year journey of 'Bandersnatch'. *The Hollywood Reporter*. 28 December. Available at: www.hollywoodreporter.com/live-feed/black-mirror-bandersnatch-netflixs-interactive-film-explained-1171486

Tai, C. (2020). Exploding the myths behind K-pop. *The Guardian*, 29 March. Available at: www.theguardian.com/global/2020/mar/29/behind-k-pops-perfect-smiles-and-dance-routines-are-tales-of-sexism-and-abuse

Tait, A. (2017). The march of the micro-influencers: why your friends are promoting toothpaste. *New Statesman*. 5 April. Available at: www.newstatesman.com/science-tech/social-media/2017/04/march-micro-influencers-why-your-friends-are-promoting-toothpaste

Taylor, C. (2019). Why Advergames can be dominant on social media – lessons from Popsockets. *Forbes*. 14 May. Available at: www.forbes.com/sites/charlesrtaylor/2019/05/14/why-advergames-can-be-dominant-on-social-media-lessons-from-popsockets/#4fce6c8b2a31

Tesseras, L. (2018). A third of brands admit to not disclosing influencer partnerships. *Marketing Week*. 14 November. Available at: www.marketingweek.com/influencer-marketing-partnerships/

Two Lights: Relúmĭno (2017). YouTube video, added by Samsung Electronics [Online]. Available at: www.youtube.com/watch?v=3y5zBY96Mio

Wise, K., Bolls, P. D., Kim, H., Venkataraman, A., and Meyer, R. (2008). Enjoyment of advergames and brand attitudes. *Journal of Interactive Advertising*. **9**(1): 27–36

Yoon, K-B. (2019). 지금까지 이런 광고음악은 없었다… CM송도 고퀄리티 시대. *Sports World*. 5 March. Available at: https://entertain.naver.com/read?oid=396&aid=0000505128

4   Issues, challenges, and prospects

> The changes we've managed to bring have created a better and more connected world. But for all the good we've achieved, the web has evolved into an engine of inequity and division; swayed by powerful forces who use it for their own agendas.
>
> (Sir Tim Berners-Lee, 2018)

Having discussed recent examples of branded entertainment in Korea, this chapter addresses a range of critical issues concerning ethics, regulation, and consumer literacy. As we have seen in the previous chapters, brands use branded entertainment to engage with consumers in an alternative and non-traditional way, mostly through digital content. Although branded entertainment can be distributed through traditional media, it is particularly prevalent through the internet (Hudson and Hudson, 2006; Zhang, Sung, and Lee, 2010). As the digital world is rapidly developing, there is growing concern in Korea that there are gaps in regulation and that existing regulations are fragmented and poorly enforced online (Yu, 2018; Song, 2019). This chapter examines challenges for the branded entertainment industry and critical issues for the wider society in Korea. The manner in which these issues are identified and addressed in Korea also offers important lessons for the governance of branded content in other societies.

Challenges in regulating branded entertainment

The regulation of digital content in Korea is currently carried out by multiple governmental agencies and industry self-regulatory bodies. The key government and statutory regulatory agencies are as follows: the Korea Communication Commission (KCC), the Korea Fair Trade Commission (KFTC), the Ministry of Health and Welfare, the Korea

Communications Standards Commission, and the Korea Media Rating Board (Kwon, 2018). The self-regulatory bodies include the Korea Online Ad Association (KOA), the Korea Internet Self-governance Organisation (KISO), and the Korea Internet Advertising Foundation. In addition, as discussed in Chapter 1, the Korea Internet & Security Agency (KISA) also operates the Online Advertising Dispute Mediation Committee in order to deal with the growing number of small disputes in online advertising (Kwon, 2018). There is also a Korea Community Media Foundation (KCMF), a quasi-government agency under the KCC, operating community media centres in metropolitan cities in Korea (KCMF, 2016).

Across the ten organisations listed above, the current regulations apply primarily to traditional methods of product placement, while no legislation or a code of conduct mentions the term 'branded entertainment'. As discussed in Chapter 2, the *Broadcasting Act* (Article 73-2) defines product placements as 'commercials that expose products, trademarks, names or logos of companies or services and others within broadcast programmes' (Korea Ministry of Government Legislation, 2020). Since product placement was allowed in terrestrial broadcasting and cable channels in Korea in January 2010, there have been ongoing debates about regulation of product placement (Han and Moon, 2015). There are no restrictions on product placement in films. The current enforcement ordinance of the *Broadcasting Act* (Article 47) states that product placement 'should not interfere with the flow of viewing', but there is an exception when it is *inevitable* due to the nature, development of contents, and the composition of the programme (Korea Communications Standards Commission, 2019) (author's emphasis). The product name, commercial expressions, sounds, or images, reminiscent of product placement, or any description of features and advantages need to be specifically exposed and mentioned through subtitles, audio, or props. However, the definition of the 'inevitable' is not clear, nor is there any explanation about fees or other considerations in exchange for product placement. Thus, the lack of definition and clear guidance in legislation in Korea makes it difficult to regulate product placement and branded entertainment effectively.

According to the current enforcement ordinance of the *Broadcasting Act* (Article 47), 'the *Regulation on Broadcasting Advertising Deliberation* is applied to the misrepresentation, exaggeration, and compliance with mandatory labelling of commercial expressions through exposure to product placements (or indirectly advertised products)' (Korea Communications Standards Commission, 2019). However, compliance with mandatory labelling is also regulated by the KFTC. Prohibited unfair labelling or advertising is classified into four types by the KFTC: first, false or exaggerated labelling or advertising; second, deceptive labelling or advertising; third, unfairly comparative labelling or advertising; fourth, slanderous labelling or advertising (KFTC, 2017). Under the *Act on Unfair Labelling and Advertising*, the KFTC defines advertising as 'activities that are conducted to widely publicise the contents of a commodity, terms and conditions of transactions to consumers through newspapers, broadcasting, magazines, samples, Internet, or signboards' (KFTC, 2017). Here, it is important to acknowledge that whereas the relevant clauses in the *Broadcasting Act* for product placement concern terrestrial broadcasting and cable channels only, the KFTC's guidelines include measures for the internet.

There are also industry self-regulatory bodies such as the Korea Online Ad Association (KOA), the Korea Internet Self-governance Organisation (KISO), and the Korea Internet Advertising Foundation. However, it is still difficult to regulate digital content due to legal loopholes in the system (Kwon, 2018). For example, the Korea Communications Standards Commission sanctioned 14 cases on the grounds of misleading or excessive use of product placement, but they were all from domestic terrestrial broadcasting channels (Kim, 2019).

The KFTC established the rules and guidelines for the examination of internet advertisements (2016a), advertising of recommendation and guarantee (2016b), and deceptive labelling and advertising (2016c), which are particularly relevant for the branded entertainment industry in Korea. The *Guidelines for the examination of advertising of recommendation and guarantee* (2016a) state that 'advertising using personal experiences or the context of recommendation or guarantee by an expert, celebrity or organisation should not cause any damage'. A 'celebrity' is defined as someone who 'is well known to consumers or can influence consumers via TV, internet or social networking service (SNS)': for example, 'those who work in entertainment, culture, art, sports, medical profession, educators, clergy, and bloggers'. It is worth noting that bloggers are recognised as celebrities since some branded entertainment formats such as reality and entertainment shows frequently feature bloggers and their recommendations. However, what distinguishes bloggers from micro-bloggers is vague. In addition, the nature of 'damage' is not specified in the guidelines, but there are exemplars of potential damage: for example, a blogger recommends a diet food which is claimed to be based on personal experiences or a medical expert's opinion; however, it turns out to be misrepresentation or exaggeration. These vague terms and the absence of clear indicators about what qualifies experts or celebrities make it difficult for market actors, complainants, regulators, or a court to determine the scope of this regulatory framework.

Under the current *Act on Fair Labelling and Advertising* (KFTC, 2017), 'material facts should be disclosed in labelling or advertising [...] which may affect consumers' choice of purchase' and 'such material facts and methods in labelling and advertising should be mandatorily included in the business operator's labelling and advertising, so as to expand the scope of information that will be provided to consumers for reasonable selection of commodities' (Article 4).

> The major material facts that shall be disclosed are the facts the omission of which in labelling or advertising have frequently caused damage to consumers, likely to decisively affect consumers' choice of purchase or likely to be harmful to human life or body, or other facts that are likely to severely interfere with consumers' reasonable choice or severely disturb the order of fair trade.
>
> (Article 4 (1) 1 and 2, the Act on Fair Labelling and Advertising, KFTC, 2017)

Again, the ambiguity of terms such as 'damage', 'severely interfere or disturb', and 'reasonable choice' makes it difficult for market actors, consumers, and regulators to agree on the same interpretation. The KFTC established the following phrases to be included in sponsored content using a recommendation or guarantee:

1. In exchange for this promotion, I have received financial rewards (e.g. cash, vouchers, commission, or free gifts)
2. This content is 'sponsored' or 'paid-for' advertising; #spon or #ad (Article 5 (1), KFTC, 2016b)

However, the above recommendations are not always adhered to, especially in the field of influencer marketing on social media (Suk, 2019). The KFTC investigated various Instagram advertisements from 2017 to 2019 in cosmetics, small electrical appliances, and diet supplements, and fined seven companies a total of £174,490 for 4,177 cases of sponsored content without any disclosure causing damage to consumers (KFTC, 2019). This was the first case of strict sanctions imposed by the KFTC for influencer marketing (Suk, 2019). In April 2020, the KFTC provided the *Administrative Notice* of the revision of the guidelines for advertising based on recommendations and guarantees (KFTC, 2020). While there is an ongoing effort to polish guidance and recommendations by regulators, it is critical that market actors adhere to the provided rules and recommendations by adding clear and prominent identifiers on their social media posts. Equally importantly, consumers need to be equipped with media literacy so that they can distinguish social media content that is not immediately clear to them as marketing communications.

Media literacy has been promoted as an important means of equipping people with the skills to decode media and marketing communications (Hardy, 2010: 260). In Korea, there are diverse groups involved in media literacy education, ranging from non-profit organisations, governmental agencies, educators, media producers, activists, and scholars to the general public (Yoon, Jeong, and Kim, 2019). In the late 1990s, the Korea Agency for Digital Opportunity & Promotion (KADO) was set up to increase access to the internet and supply digital literacy training to over 10 million inhabitants to be internet-ready (Mills, 2018). Under the *Broadcasting Act* Article 9(2), the Korea Communications Commission established Community Media Centres to provide media education: the first centre opened in Busan in 2005, and as of April 2020, there were seven centres across the country (Community Media Foundation, 2020). The Community Media Centres offer media literacy programmes as well as the free rental of broadcasting production facilities and equipment. In September 2019, front-line teachers also set up the Korean Association of Teachers of Media Literacy to incorporate media literacy skills into state education. At the same time, there have also been industry initiatives: for example, electronics and telecommunications companies such as Samsung, LG, KT, and SKT provide experiential learning opportunities for the general public (Mills, 2018). Google also launched a pilot programme to bring digital and media literacy skills to secondary school students in Seoul and Gyeonggi provinces in Korea (Fuller, 2019). Google's *Campus Seoul* has existed since 2015, but it is more geared towards entrepreneurs rather than literacy education (Grove, 2015).

Despite the government media literacy strategies and industry initiatives, critics have called for more support to fund media and digital literacy education for those most in need (Oh et al., 2018: 91). One of the most vulnerable groups is the elderly. In Korea, as of 2018, internet users among older adults (65+) accounted for 59.9 per cent and smartphone adoption among the same cohort for 65.2 per cent, both of which are significantly lower than the rest of the population (National Information Society Agency, 2018). A recent study finds that while the digital divide is closing for young cohorts, it is still an issue for older people in Korea (Yoon, Lee, and Lee, 2019). It also reveals that information and communications technology (ICT) training plays a significant role in older people's digital literacy.[1] Although this study focuses on a small sample of seven community centres in Seoul, with a particular focus on digital literacy and smartphones, it sheds light on the importance of the educative role played by the government and by the communities.

This is not to say that media literacy education should be limited to older adults. As discussed in Chapter 3, there are important issues such as authenticity, creative autonomy, and consumer awareness when it comes to increasingly close working relationships between entertainment agencies, K-pop idols, the media, and marketing industries. Kang (2017: 136) argues that the K-pop 'idol' label has negative associations for the press and the general public that K-pop idols are mass-produced by entertainment companies and thus lack authenticity; however, at the same time, they have gained social legitimacy as an exportable commodity. There exists criticism regarding the subculture, not just the mainstream idol star system: for example, Hare and Baker (2017: 10) found that commodification dominates authenticity in the Korean hip-hop scene. One K-pop blogger has commented on the commercialisation of the industry, describing K-pop as being on the verge of becoming advertising (Johnson, 2015). Some formats of branded entertainment (e.g. entertainment/reality shows and creator contents) are more difficult for viewers to identify as marketing communications. Consumers, young or old, can learn to think critically via media and digital literacy education.

Challenges in evaluating branded entertainment

Based on the previous discussion of the societal concerns, this section examines those of greater importance from an industry perspective. The principal challenges from an industry perspective are to evaluate, and demonstrate to clients, the promotional effectiveness of branded content campaigns. As we have seen in the previous chapters, what constitutes branded entertainment is very diverse. This makes it difficult to measure and evaluate the outcome. In addition, it is often a part of a wider marketing campaign, and therefore, isolating its success can be difficult.

Traditional product placement has been studied frequently in terms of effectiveness by the way the placement is made, meaning that most of the results show how the characteristics of a brand placement affect its effectiveness (Lehu and Bressoud, 2008: 1084). For example, Balasubramanian, Karrh, and Patwardhan (2006) developed an integrative conceptual model to capture audience responses to product placement across four components: execution/stimulus factors, individual-specific factors, processing depth, and message outcomes that reflect placement effectiveness.[2] Lehu and Bressoud (2008) also explored viewers' reactions to product placement in films, using a sample of 3,532 French viewers. They found that first viewing the movie at the cinema improves brand placement recall, and that brand placement efficiency also increases with the second viewing (e.g. watching the same movie at home on DVD).

More recently, there have been attempts from academia to establish a systematic evaluation system for branded entertainment in the Western context (see Wright 2012; Fulgoni, Pettit, and Lipsman, 2017). These studies were based on an experimental design whereby the respondents were exposed to the campaign, or elements of it, in a controlled way. In a similar vein, Choi et al. (2018) examined online branded entertainment videos in terms of brand prominence, brand disclosure timing, and the consumer's decision to share the video. They conducted a 2 (brand prominence: prominent vs. subtle) x 2 (brand disclosure timing: pre- vs. post-disclosure) between-subject eye-tracking experiment in a research lab (Choi et al. 2018: 23). The results suggested that the effect of pre-disclosure on viewer's sharing intention of branded entertainment video content is likely to differ depending on the level of brand prominence, while the effect of post-disclosure seems more independent from the brand prominence in the content. This experiment used a brand (Red Bull) familiar to the participants who were undergraduate students, with a particular focus on brand logos. Although it does not offer a comprehensive tool to measure effectiveness, it has practical implications in terms of the regulation of sponsorship disclosure. Using the same line of research methodology (2x2 lab experiment), Bang et al. (2020) examined the overall effect of a cross-category brand alliance[3] in branded entertainment content. Based on a 2 (alliance exclusivity: alliance with a single brand vs. alliance with multiple brands) x 2 (presentation style: massing vs. spacing) between-subjects design, they found that the mere co-appearance of multiple brands in branded entertainment cannot guarantee a leveraging effect (Bang et al., 2020: 478). This experiment measured only brand familiarity and brand attitudes regarding well-established brands.

While some academic research has contributed to assessing marketing effectiveness, industry specialist tools are either developed in-house by agencies or by specialist services (intermediaries) and sold to agencies to identify and measure brand placements. For example, in the United Kingdom, the Branded content evaluation system (Bces) was developed by the United Kingdom's Branded Content Marketing Association (BCMA) in collaboration with OTX and Pointlogic (advertising and planning research companies) in 2009 (BCMA, 2009). This was proposed as a way of evaluating the return on investment (ROI), focusing on how branded content campaigns perform against key brand metrics (*Marketing Week*, 2009).

The aforementioned models and findings are primarily based on lab experiments or case studies, with a particular focus on specific aspects of branded entertainment. Hence, the key challenge in evaluating the effectiveness of branded entertainment is that existing measurement tools have limited applicability. Indeed, as argued by Hardy (2018: 117), the durability of branded content (which branded entertainment belongs to) will depend on effective measurement tools that convince clients of longer-term benefits for ROI. However, there are additional challenges to demonstrating and measuring ROI for clients. Industry reports indicate that marketers claim that social media and content marketing are among the most difficult channels to measure for ROI (Miliopoulou, 2019: 493). Furthermore, much branded content is strongest at building awareness early in the customer journey to purchase, and therefore the ROI may be much less immediate than other marketing communications campaigns (Dzamic and Kirby, 2018). Another challenge concerns scaling branded content production (Taylor, 2019). Pressure on publishers and content creators to consistently produce original content, and cost implications are a major obstacle for marketers to maintain effective branded entertainment campaigns (Lee, 2019). There are thus various challenges for the branded entertainment industry.

Prospects

Based on the primary research and analysis, this section outlines three key issues regarding the prospects for branded entertainment in Korea. First, the viability of certain branded entertainment formats, especially webtoons, is one of the important factors when it comes to the prospects *for* industry. Due to an insufficient revenue policy, platforms and webtoonists have become heavily reliant on product placement and branded entertainment. As discussed in Chapter 1, the issue of exploitation has been raised concerning the relationship between platform and labour. As platform operators are fully in charge of a platform's techno-economic development, the power relations among platform operators, end users, and complementors are extremely volatile and inherently asymmetrical (Poell, Nieborg, and van Dijck, 2019). This influences the editorial direction and creative autonomy of webtoonists (Kim and Yu, 2019). Concerns over the effects of platformisation on creative labour have been shared by those in the media and creative industries as well as various governmental agencies. In an interview with *OhMyNews*, Lee Hyun-Se, a Korean first-generation cartoonist, lamented that 'in Korea, comics (inclusive of webtoons) are seen more as business not as culture' (Jung, 2019). Poor working conditions for Korean webtoonists have been under scrutiny by the domestic media (Jung, 2017; Noh, 2018; Kang, 2019). In response to this, guidelines for fair contracts were introduced by the Ministry of Culture, Sports and Tourism, the Korea Creative Content Agency (KOCCA), and the Korea Cartoonist Association in December 2019 (KOCCA, 2019). In addition, several small- and medium-sized webtoon platforms with a more 'creator-centred incubating policy' have emerged (Kim and Yu, 2019: 7). From a brand's perspective, small- and medium-sized brands can benefit from a wider range of platforms for more competitive pricing to implement their branded entertainment strategies.

Secondly, in order to have effective and timely policymaking and legislation, there needs to be a more streamlined approach, with fewer organisations involved. As discussed, there are currently multiple governmental agencies and industry self-regulatory bodies which are involved in advertising regulation in Korea. Several scholars have already proposed to simplify the process regarding the regulation of product placement and branded entertainment. Han and Moon (2015: 140) argued that a centralised regulatory procedure would facilitate more efficient resourcing of a trained workforce to deal with the examination of issues and complaints, while protecting marketers and consumers. Kwon (2018: 11) also proposed to streamline the process by benchmarking the collaborative model between the Korea Internet & Security Agency and the KFTC. These two organisations established the Online Advertising Dispute Mediation Committee to deal with small disputes quickly. According to the Korea Internet & Security Agency, there were 1,279 cases of online advertising-related disputes in 2016 alone, 84 per cent of which were small claims under 2,000,000 Korean won (approx. £1,322) (Kwon, 2018: 2). Disputes between small businesses and advertising/media agencies about search advertising contracts account for 55 per cent, followed by viral marketing (e.g. blog, SNS)-related disputes accounting for 22 per cent, of all the disputes (Korea Internet & Security Agency, 2016). Therefore, quick processing and mediation by the Committee could benefit small- and medium-sized marketers and prevent potential damage to consumers. Although 'one-stop service' for marketers or consumers may not be realistic due to the complex nature of disputes and complaints, a more streamlined and centralised approach would benefit market actors, regulators, and society. In response to the fast-evolving digital economy, collaboration between industry self-regulatory bodies and governmental agencies increases efficiency in regulation.

Lastly, consumer media literacy is increasingly more important in the digital age. Yu (2018: 205) points out that the lack of media literacy education and inefficient regulation results in various societal and ethical problems in Korea. Livingstone (2018) states that media literacy seems to be 'everyone's favourite solution to the problems of regulation', yet 'what media literacy includes is a moving target'. Indeed, online privacy literacy education is of growing importance. In particular, children are often exposed to data disclosure requests from e-service providers and yet, they may not always be aware of the commercial value of their data and the associated privacy risks (Desimpelaerea, Huddersa, and van de Sompela, 2020). A recent study investigated how privacy literacy training increases children's (aged 9–13 years) privacy literacy, influencing their online disclosure behaviour (Desimpelaerea, Huddersa, and van de Sompela, 2020). Their findings show that training enhances children's general understanding of data practices and helps children better protect their privacy, including holding back and fabricating personal information, as well as identifying low privacy risks. Interestingly, those who have enhanced privacy literacy show more negative brand responses.

Any media literacy strategy requires sustained attention, resources, and commitment to education, to curriculum development, to teacher training, to research and evaluation (Livingstone, 2018). It was promising to see the Korean Association of Teachers of Media Literacy be established in 2019. We have also seen industry initiatives in this area. It is, however, crucial for educators, regulators, and consumers to understand the notion of media literacy as a moving target and update curriculum (e.g. schools, the Korea Community Media Foundation) accordingly.

Concluding remarks

The goal of this book has been to advance the explanation and understanding of branded entertainment in Korea. It also examined critical issues such as ethics, regulation, and consumer literacy to address the impact and implications of media and marketing integration for consumers and societies. This new form of promotional communication continues to evolve but not without critical concerns and challenges. We have seen how closely brands have been working with the Korean pop culture industry to engage with consumers in domestic, regional, and global contexts. For the last two decades, the Korean wave and advanced digital infrastructure has accelerated the growth of branded entertainment; however, as we have seen in the previous chapters, authenticity and creative autonomy were not always secured in the process, especially in the convergence of brands and entertainment. An examination of recent examples of branded entertainment shows that engagement and participation are crucial elements in branded entertainment. Participatory culture is a prerequisite condition for effective branded entertainment.

Nowadays 'every company is a media company ("EC = MC") because every company publishes to its customers, its staff, its neighbours and its communities' (Foremski, 2009). However, not every company will make a good media company because we live in a complicated world of media technologies such as a multiplatform, multichannel, micro-media world, with the trend moving towards ever greater media fragmentation (Foremski, 2010). The rise of branded entertainment illustrates that brands are not just becoming publishers but entertainers (Rose, 2013). This is the reason why the discussion of branded entertainment becomes much more important, as every company needs to know how to use all the media technologies at its disposal. Understanding this 'EC = MC' formula moves beyond social media. In an era of the convergence of media and marketing integration, a new promotional communication such as branded entertainment could be an essential tool for brand management in every company.

Branded entertainment illustrates the way that marketers have sought to co-link entertainment content with new technological infrastructures to give brands greater *credibility, interactivity*, and *depth of appeal*. With the shift towards digital content consumption, brands need to share value-added stories that build *trust* to increase consumer engagement. It is true that branded entertainment provides alternative ways to engage with consumers, but this strategy should not be treated as a way to elude regulation. Media and marketing industries need to adhere to rules and guidelines; and government agencies and self-regulatory bodies should keep up to date with the developments in the industry, eliminating any legal loopholes and caveats in the system. Media literacy education in a broad sense should be in place not just through industry initiatives but also through government and grassroots support. Consumers also need to be proactive to protect their own privacy and rights while improving their literacy skills to identify marketing communications as such. Thus, for branded entertainment to evolve and thrive as an ethical and sustainable marketing strategy, all the parties involved need to play their parts regardless of their own agendas.

Notes

1 Based on a face-to-face, researcher-assisted questionnaire survey with 372 people, over 60, at seven community centres in Seoul in 2018, Yoon, Lee, and Lee (2019) found that those who took ICT training courses at community centres showed a higher smartphone usage level (M = 126 minutes) than those who did not have any training (M = 81 minutes), and a higher level of literacy and competence in using various types of smartphone functions.
2 This model depicts four components: execution/stimulus factors (e.g. programme type, execution flexibility, opportunity to process, placement modality, placement priming); individual-specific factors (e.g. brand familiarity, judgment of placement fit, attitudes towards placements, involvement/connectedness with program); processing depth (degree of conscious processing); and message outcomes that reflect placement effectiveness. Here, execution and individual factors influence processing depth, which in turn impacts message outcomes. These outcomes are organised around the hierarchy-of-effects model into three broad categories: cognition (e.g. memory-related measures such as recognition and recall); affect (e.g. attitudes); and conation (e.g. purchase intention, purchase behaviour) (Balasubramanian, Karrh, and Patwardhan, 2006: 115).
3 Rodrigue and Biswas (2004) suggest that brand alliance can be defined as two types: joint promotion involving the promotion of complementary use; and the ingredient brand alliance involving an integration of two products, one of which cannot be consumed without consuming the other.

Bibliography

Balasubramanian, S. K., Karrh, J. A., and Patwardhan, H. (2006). Audience response to product placements: an integrative framework and future research agenda. *Journal of Advertising*. **35**(3), 115–141.

Bang, H., Choi, D., Baek, T. H., Oh, S. D., and Kim, Y. (2020). Leveraged brand evaluations in branded entertainment: effects of alliance exclusivity and presentation style. *International Journal of Advertising*. **39**(4), 466–485.

Berners-Lee, T. (2018). 'One Small Step for the Web…', *Medium*, 29 September. Available at: https://medium.com/timberners_lee/onesmall-step-for-the-web-87f92217d085

Branded Content Marketing Association (BCMA) (2009). *Branded content evaluation system (Bces)*, October. Available at: www.thebcma.info/oldsite-uploads/bces-summary2.pdf

Choi, D., Bang, H., Wojdynski, B. W., Lee, Y-I., and Keib, K. M. (2018). How brand disclosure timing and brand prominence influence consumer's intention to share branded entertainment content. *Journal of Interactive Marketing*. **42**, 18–31.

Community Media Foundation (2020). 미디어 리터러시: 방송시설 및 장비지원', 시청자 미디어재단. Available at: https://kcmf.or.kr/cms/board/content.php?menuIdx=34

Desimpelaerea, L., Huddersa, L., and van de Sompela, D. (2020). Knowledge as a strategy for privacy protection: how a privacy literacy training affects children's online disclosure behaviour. *Computers in Human Behaviour.* **110**, 106382. Available at: https://www.sciencedirect.com/science/article/abs/pii/S0747563220301357

Dzamic, L., and Kirby, J. (2018). *Definitive guide to strategic content marketing: perspectives, issues, challenges and solutions.* London and New York: Kogan Page.

Einstein, M. (2016). *Black ops advertising: native ads, content marketing, and the covert world of the digital sell.* New York and London: OR Books.

Foremski, T. (2009). Every company is a media company. *ZDNet.* 22 August. Available at: www.zdnet.com/article/every-company-is-a-media-company/

Foremski, T. (2010). Welcome – when every company is a media company… March. Available at: www.everycompanyisamediacompany.com/every-company-is-a-media-/2010/03/welcome-when-every-company-is-a-media-company.html#more

Fulgoni, G., Pettit, R., and Lipsman, A. (2017). Measuring the effectiveness of branded content across television and digital platforms: how to align with traditional marketing metrics while capturing what makes branded content unique. *Journal of Advertising Research.* **57**(4), 362–367.

Fuller, J. (2019). Bringing digital and media literacy education to more schools in Korea. *Google the Keyword.* Available at: www.blog.google/outreach-initiatives/google-org/digital-and-media-literacy-education-korea/

Geum, J-K. (2019). 미디어 비판적 이해 제대로 가르치자' 교사들 뭉쳤다. *Media Today.* 24 September. Available at: https://n.news.naver.com/article/006/0000098880

Grove, M. (2015). Come start something with us at Campus Seoul. *Google the Keyword.* Available at: https://blog.google/topics/google-asia/come-start-something-with-us-at-campus/

Han, K-H., and Moon, J-H. (2015). 국내 간접광고 규제의 개선방향에 관한 고찰: 해외의 간접광고 규제 사례 분석을 토대로', *광고연구.* Spring, **104**, 109–146.

Hardy, J. (2010). Cross-Media Promotion. New York: Peter Lang.

Hardy, J. (2018). Branded content: media and marketing integration. In: J. Hardy, H. Powell, and I. Macrury, eds. *Advertising Handbook.* 4th ed. Abingdon and New York: Routledge, pp. 102–122.

Hare, S., and Baker, A. (2017). Keepin' it real: authenticity, commercialization, and the media in Korean hip hop. *Sage Open.* April–June, **7**(2), 1–12.

Hudson, S., and Hudson, D. (2006). Branded entertainment: a new advertising technique or product placement in disguise. *Journal of Marketing Management.* **22**(5), 489–504.

Johnson, M. (2015). The long arm of product placement (꼬리가 긴 PPL 케이팝이 CF 가 될 때). *The Mind Reels.* 29 July. Available at: https://blog.mjohnso.com/post/125369320166/the-long-arm-of-product-placement

Jung, M-K. (2017). 샤워하다 쓰러지고, 공황장애… 웹툰작가들 노동환경 심각. *Media Today 미디어오늘.* 25 June. Available at: www.mediatoday.co.kr/news/articleView.html?idxno=137461

Jung, S-H. (2019). 이현세 악플도 반기는 웹툰계... 정말 위험합니다. *OhMyNews*. 29 June. Available at: www.ohmynews.com/NWS_Web/View/at_pg.aspx?CNTN_CD=A0002549777

Kang, J. M. (2017). Rediscovering the idols: K-pop idols behind the mask. *Celebrity Studies*. **8**(1), 136–141.

Kang, Y-S. (2019). [한국에서 웹툰작가로 산다는 것] 불공정 계약이란 걸 알아도 서명할 수밖에 없어요. *Labour Today* 매일노동뉴스. 22 April. Available at: www.labortoday.co.kr/news/articleView.html?idxno=158005

Kim, J-C. (2019). *한국의 미디어 법제와 정책해설 2*. Seoul: Communication Books.

Kim, J-H., and Yu, J. (2019). Platformizing webtoons: the impact on creative and digital labour in South Korea. *Social Media + Society*. October–December, 1–11.

Kim, B-C., Choi, Y-H., Kim, H-C., Kim, Y-M., Kim, J-R., Bae, J-Y., and An, J-A. (2018). 브랜드인가, 콘텐츠인가?: 브랜디드 콘텐츠의 현재와 미래. *Proceedings of Korea Advertising Society 'Crossing the Boundaries: Advertising in a Polynominal Media Ecology'*. Spring Conference. 7 April. Korea University, Seoul. pp. 179–188.

Korea Communications Commission (KCC) (2019). '방통위, 2019 미디어,정보 리터러시 국제 컨퍼런스 개최', Press Release, 28 November.

Korea Communications Standards Commission (2019). 방송심의에 관한 규정. 27 September. 국가법령정보센터. Available at: www.law.go.kr/%ED%96%89%EC%A0%95%EA%B7%9C%EC%B9%99/%EB%B0%A9%EC%86%A1%EC%8B%AC%EC%9D%98%EC%97%90%20%EA%B4%80%ED%95%9C%20%EA%B7%9C%EC%A0%95

Korea Community Media Foundation (KCMF) (2016). 알기쉬운 방송광고 모니터링 기준. 25 August. Available at: https://kcmf.or.kr/cms/lib/view2.php?idx=7063

Korea Creative Content Agency (KOCCA) (2014), 웹툰산업의 구조적 문제점과 개선방안. 30 June. Available at: www.kocca.kr/cop/bbs/view/B0000141/1822409.do?menuNo=200898

Korea Creative Content Agency (KOCCA) (2019). 만화.웹툰 공정계약 가이드. 30 December. Available at: www.kocca.kr/cop/bbs/view/B0000147/1841426.do?searchCnd=1&searchWrd=%EC%9B%B9%ED%88%B0&cateTp1=&cateTp2=&useAt=&menuNo=201825&categorys=0&subcate=0&cateCode=&type=&instNo=0&questionTp=&uf_Setting=&recovery=&option1=&option2=&year=&categoryCOM062=&categoryCOM063=&categoryCOM208=&categoryInst=&morePage=&delCode=0&qtp=&pageIndex=1#

Korea Fair Trade Commission (KFTC) (2016a). *Guidelines for Examination of Internet Advertisements*. The Fair Trade Commission Established Rule No. 272, 23 December. Korea Fair Trade Commission (Consumer Safety & Information Division).

Korea Fair Trade Commission (KFTC) (2016b). *추천, 보증 등에 관한 표시, 광고 심사지침*, The Fair Trade Commission Established Rule No. 271, 23 December. Korea Fair Trade Commission (Consumer Safety & Information Division).

Korea Fair Trade Commission (KFTC) (2016c). *Guidelines for Examination of Deceptive Labelling and Advertising*. Established Rule of Fair Trade Commission No. 268, 23 December. Korea Fair Trade Commission (Consumer Safety & Information Division).

Korea Fair Trade Commission (KFTC) (2017). *Act on Fair Labelling and Advertising*. Act No. 15142, 28 November. Partial Amendment. Korea Fair Trade Commission (Consumer Safety & Information Division).

Korea Fair Trade Commission (KFTC) (2019). 보도: 표시광고법 위반 7개사 제재. 25 November. Available at: www.ftc.go.kr/www/selectReportUserView. do?key=10&rpttype=1&report_data_no=8370

Korea Fair Trade Commission (KFTC) (2020). \추천, 보증 등에 관한 표시, 광고 심사지침 개정안 행정예고. 29 April. Available at: www.ftc.go.kr/www/ selectReportUserView.do?key=10&rpttype=1&report_data_no=8545

Korea Internet & Security Agency (2016). 온라인광고 분쟁조정 사례집 *Online Advertising Dispute Case Studies*. Seoul.

Korea Ministry of Government Legislation (2020). *Broadcasting Act*. 9 April. Available at: www.law.go.kr

Kwon, Y-K. (2018). 온라인 광고 관련 경쟁법 이슈와 시사점', 공정거래 이슈브리핑. Korea Fair Trade Mediation Agency 한국공정거래조정원.

Lee, S-K. (2019). [브랜드가 광고를 대하는 올바른 자세]] 브랜디드 콘텐츠의 이해. 4 June. Available at: https://ppss.kr/archives/196612

Lehu, J-M., and Bressoud, E. (2008). Effectiveness of brand placement: new insights about viewers. *Journal of Business Research*. 61, 1083–1090.

Livingstone, S. (2018). Media literacy – everyone's favourite solution to the problems of regulation. LSE Blog. Available at: https://blogs.lse. ac.uk/medialse/2018/05/08/media-literacy-everyones-favourite-solution-to-the-problems-of-regulation/

Marketing Week (2009). Value of branded content can be measured. 1 January. Available at: www.marketingweek.com/value-of-branded-content-can-be-measured/

Miliopoulou, G-Z. (2019). Revisiting product classification to examine content marketing practices. *Journal of Research in Interactive Marketing*. 13(4), 492–508.

Mills, T. (2018). How the Republic of Korea became a world ICT leader. *International Telecommunication Union (ITU) News*. 12 February. Available at: https://news. itu.int/republic-korea-leader-information-communication-technologies/

National Information Society Agency (2018). *National Informatisation White Paper*, National Information Society Agency. Korea.

Noh, J-H. (2018). 웹툰 강국 '대한민국'에서 웹툰 작가들이 착취당하는 법. *JoongAng Daily* 중앙일보, 30 January. Available at: https://news.joins.com/ article/22331154

Oh, M-R., Kang, W-S., Kim, Y-C., Baek, J-H., Yu, C-J., Lee S-H., and Lee, J-E. (2018). 공유가치창출을 위한 그린 광고의 이론 및 사례 (Green ad toward 'creating shared value'). *Proceedings of Korea Advertising Society 'Crossing the Boundaries: Advertising in a Polynominal Media Ecology'*. Spring Conference, 7 April. Korea University, Seoul. pp. 76–116.

Poell, T., Nieborg, D., and van Dijck, J. (2019). Platformisation. *Internet Policy Review*. **8**(4), 1–13.

Rodrigue, C. S., and Biswas, A. (2004). Brand alliance dependency and exclusivity: an empirical investigation. *Journal of Product and Brand Management*. **13**(7), 477–487.

Rose, J. (2013). Let me entertain you: the rise of branded entertainment. The Guardian. 26 September. Available at: www.theguardian.com/media-network/2013/sep/26/branded-entertainment-content-marketing

Song, H-Y. (2019). 몰입형 기술이 만들어낸 디지털 현실에 대한 안전 규제 필요성. Korea Communications Agency Media Issue & Trend. **26**, 84–99.

Suk, M-S. (2019). 후기? 알고보니 광고... 공정위, SNS 인플루언서 통한 광고 첫 제재. *KBS News*. 25 November. Available at: https://news.kbs.co.kr/news/view.do?ncd=4330510

Taylor, M. (2019). Reduce, reuse, refocus: How to scale your branded content operation. *Digital Content Next*. 12 April. Available at: https://digitalcontentnext.org/blog/2019/04/12/reduce-reuse-refocus-how-to-scale-your-branded-content-operation/

Wright, I. (2012). Entertainment evaluation. *Admap*. February.

Yoon, H., Lee, G-O., and Lee, S-Y. (2019). Digital divide: a case of South Korean older adults. Presentation, United Nations Economic and Social Commission of Asia and the Pacific (ESCAP), Asia-Pacific Information Superhighway Steering Committee and WSIS Regional Review. 27 August. Bangkok, Thailand.

Yoon, J., Jeong, H-S., and Kim, A. (2019). Media literacy in South Korea. *The International Encyclopedia of Media Literacy*. published online 9 May. John Wiley & Sons.

Yu, H-J., and Ji, E-J. (2018). 웹툰 PPL, 호평과 혹평 가르는 요인. *The PR News*. 17 October. Available at: www.the-pr.co.kr/news/articleView.html?idxno=41170

Yu, S-W. (2018). 디지털 커뮤니케이션과 콘텐츠: 신뢰와 PR의 윤리적 이슈. In: S-S. Cho, Y-N. Lee, Y-W. Kim, J-Y. Kim, S-W. Yu, W-J. Jung, J-H. Choi, and H-L. Choi, eds. *디지털 사회와 PR 윤리*, Seoul: Communication Books.

Zhang, J., Sung, Y., and Lee, W-N. (2010). To play or not to play: an exploratory content analysis of branded entertainment in Facebook. *American Journal of Business*. **25**(1), 53–64.

Index

Note: Page numbers in **bold** indicate tables on the corresponding pages.

Act on Fair Labelling and Advertising 61–62
advergames 49–50
Advertising in Korea 5
alcohol advertising 50–51
Allen, C. 4
An, S. 33
Anymotion project 39–40
AORB 46, 52
Artifishal 4

Baez, C. 49
Balasubramanian, S. K. 64
Bang, H. 65
Basic Law for the Promotion of the Information Society, The 7
Berners-Lee, T. 59
Big Hit Entertainment 48
Blank Corporation 48–49, 51
BMW 1, 45–46
BoA 42
Bong Joon-ho 8
branded entertainment: advergame 49–50; brand webtoons 47–48; car brands in 1; challenges in evaluating 64–66; challenges in regulating 59–64; conceptualising 30–32; conclusions on 68–69; creator contents 50–51; current state of 1–2; defined 3–5; early campaigns 39–40; future prospects for 66–68; historical context of 28–30; literature on Korean 32–34; in music/music video 40–43; new forms of digital content and its impact on 22–24; participatory culture and 51–52; research/knowledge gap in Korean advertising and 5–9; web dramas 43–45; web movies 45–47; web reality/entertainment shows 48–49
brand webtoons 47–48
Bressoud, E. 65
Broadcasting Act 8, 32, 60, 63
BTS 1, 43, 48, 52

Call Me Baby 41
car brands 1
cartoons *see* webtoons, brand
Cauberghe, V. 31, 49
Chae, M.-J. 33
Challenge, The 50
Chamisul Live 50–51, 52
Cheil Worldwide 24
Choi, D. 65
Chua, B. H. 19–20
Colgate Comedy Hour 29
conceptual models of branded entertainment 30–32
creator contents 50–51

Dagnino, G. 4, 5, 32
Dahl, S. 49
De Pelsmacker, P. 31, 49
Discovery channel 32
Donaton, S. 28

dramas, web 43–45
*Drinking Damage Prevention Action
    Plan* 51

Eagle, L. 49
East Asian popular culture
    19–21
Edison, T. 28
Einstein, M. 31–32
E Mart 44, 51
Enslin, C. 4, 5
E. T. the Extra-Terrestrial 29
evaluation of branded
    entertainment 64–66
Everyday 41

Facebook 44
5 GX Boost Park 49–50, 51
Ford Motor Co. 1

General Motors Family Party 29
God of Annual Salary 47–48, 51
GoPro 32

Han, K.-H. 67
*Handbook of Product Placement in
    the Mass Media* 31
Hanwha Chemical 47, 51
Hardy, J. 3, 4, 30, 66
Highschool Styleicon 48–49, 51
Hire, The 1, 45–46
historical context of branded
    entertainment 28–30
HiteJinro 50–51, 52
Honda 1
Honda Cog 1
Hong, D. 34
Horloyd, C. 22
Huawei 46
Hudson, D. 3, 4, 30
Hudson, S. 3, 4, 30
Hwang, J.-S. 33
Hwang, Y. 33
Hyundai Worldwide 1, 21

Identity 1, 40, 46
Internet and mobile communications
    in Korea 21–22
Iuwabuchi, K. 19–20

Jenkins, H. 51
Jeong, S.-H. 33
Jeong, Y. 6
Jin, D.-Y. 24
Jun, J. W. 33, 34, 40
Jung, S. 20
J. Walter Thomson Company 29

Kang, I. 20–21
Kang, J. M. 42
Kang, Y.-S. 64
Karrh, J. A. 64
Kia 1, 40, 45–46
Kim, Y. 6, 20
Kim Ju-Hyuk 40
Korea Advertising Review Board
    (KARB) 19
Korea Agency for Digital
    Opportunity & Promotion
    (KADO) 63
Korea Communication Commission
    (KCC) 19, 59
Korea Communication Standards
    Commission 59–60
Korea Community Media
    Foundation (KCMF) 60
Korea Creative Content Agency
    (KOCCA) 22–23, 67
Korea Electric Power Corporation
    (KEPCO) 7
Korea Fair Trade Commission
    (KFTC) 19, 59, 60–63
Korea Information Infrastructure
    (KII) 7
Korea Internet & Security Agency
    (KISA) 19, 60
Korea Internet Self-governance
    Organisation (KISO) 60, 61
Korea Mobile Telecom (KMT) 21
Korean Air 42, 52
Korean wave 19–21
Korea Online Ad Association
    (KOA) 60, 61
K-pop 20–21, 24, 40–43, 48, 64

Lavanchy-Clarke, F.-H. 28
Lee, J. 33
Lee Hyo-Ri 39
Lee Yeon-hui 40

Lehu, J.-M. 31, 65
LG 21
Lotte Chilsung 41–42
Lotte Duty Free 43–44, 51, 52
Lucky Star 1

MacDonald, P. 49
Mackay, T. 31
Maeil Bio 41, 42, 52
Mallinckrodt, V. 31
MAMAMOO 41, 52
Master Racing Challenge, The 50
Maxwell House Hour 29
media and advertising, Korea: brief
   overview of 15, **16–19**, 19; Internet
   and mobile communications 21–22;
   Korean wave in 19–21; new forms
   of digital content and its impact on
   branded entertainment and 22–24;
   public broadcasters in 15; research/
   knowledge gap in 5–9
Mercedes Benz 1
Ministry of Health and Welfare
   48, 51, 59
Mizerski, D. 31
Moon, J.-H. 67
Most Beautiful Moment in Life Pt. 0:
   Save Me, The 48
Motion Picture Association 2
Motion Picture Promotion Law 7
movies, web 45–47
multi-channel network (MCN) 34
music/music video 20–21, 24, 40–43
My Precious World 44, 51

National Health Promotion Act 51
Naver Webtoon 48, 52
Netflix 4, 32
Nieborg, D. 23
No Boundaries 1
Nongshim 45, 51

OB Beer 46, 52
O'Guinn, T. 4

Parasite 8, 45
participatory culture 51–52
Patwardhan, H. 64
Pepsi 41–42, 52

Poell, T. 23
popular culture, East Asian 19–21
product placement 28–29
Public Notice of Imposing Fine on
   Violations of the Fair Labelling and
   Advertising Act 2012 49

reality/entertainment shows 48–49
Red Bull Stratos project 32
regulation of branded entertainment,
   challenges in 59–64
Ryoo, W. 8

Samsung 21, 46, 51
Semenik, R. 4
7 First Kisses 43–44, 51, 52
Shim, D. 8, 20
Shin, I. S. 5
Shin, K. H. 5
shoppertainment 2–3
SK Telecom 21, 49–50, 51
snack culture 24
soap operas 30
So Ji-Seop 40
Some Boiling Time 44–45
Somestery Share House 45, 51, 52
Spurgeon, C. 4
Ssang Yong Motor 1, 40, 46
Sun, H.-J. 33
SuperM 42

Terblanche-Smit, M. 4, 5
true origins of pizza campaign
   40
Turow, J. 3
Twitter 1
Two Lights: *Relúmĭno* 46, 51

U-turn 1, 40, 46

van Dijck, J. 23
van Loggerenberg, M. J. C.
   4, 5

web dramas 43–45
web movies 45–47
web reality/entertainment
   shows 48–49
webtoons, brand 47–48

Wenner, L. A. 31
Wharton, C. 30
Wired 24

YDPP 41–42

YouTube 32, 41; brand webtoons
    47–48; web dramas 43–45;
    web movies 46–47; web reality/
    entertainment shows 48–49
Yu, H.-J. 68

For Product Safety Concerns and Information please contact our EU
representative GPSR@taylorandfrancis.com
Taylor & Francis Verlag GmbH, Kaufingerstraße 24, 80331 München, Germany